D0323624

Plugged

Plugged

Krissi Barr & Dan Barr

Dig out &
get the right things done

3 TOOLS
for PAR at Work

CLERISY PRESS

COPYRIGHT © 2010 by Krissi Barr and Dan Barr

ALL RIGHTS RESERVED. No portion of this book may be reproduced in any fashion, print, facsimile, or electronic, or by any method yet to be developed, without the express written permission of the copyright holder.

Published by Clerisy Press
Distributed by Publishers Group West
Printed in the United States of America
First edition, first printing

Library of Congress Cataloging-in-Publication Data

Barr, Krissi.
    Plugged : dig out & get the right things done / by
Krissi Barr and Dan Barr. — 1st ed.
        p. cm.
    ISBN-13: 978-1-57860-444-9
    ISBN-10: 1-57860-444-3
    1. Golf—Anecdotes. 2. Success in business.
    3. Management. I. Barr, Dan. II. Title.
GV967.B324 2009
796.352--dc22

                                        2009030762

Editors: Jack Heffron and Donna Poehner
Cover design: Stephen Sullivan
Interior design: Angela Wilcox
Illustrations: Todd Price/Steadfast Studios

Clerisy Press
P.O. Box 8874
Cincinnati, Ohio 45208-0874
www.clerisypress.com

Endorsements

Marshall Goldsmith, NYT and WSJ #1 best-selling author of *What Got You There Won't Get You There* and the recently published *Succession: Are You Ready?*
Using the power of story and metaphor, Krissi and Dan Barr tell a mesmerizing tale of business, golf, and overcoming challenge in their book, Plugged. *As engaging as it is practical,* Plugged *is for anyone looking to overcome today's challenges, whether they're in the boardroom or on the golf course!*

Paul Higham, Retired Chief Marketing Officer, Walmart Stores, Inc. and Principal, h factor (a marketing consulting company)
What I liked about Plugged *so much was that it was extremely human. They became obsessed with their customers. Once they got busy and genuinely concerned, they got done what they needed to and it worked. My career was built on taking out the logic and figuring out how to humanize things.* Plugged *humanized and emotionalized the rationale. And you don't have to be a golfer to get this message.*

Matthew Kelly, NYT and WSJ best-selling author of *The Dream Manager*
Life and business are not as complicated as we make them. Plugged *will help you clarify what matters most and place it at the center of your life and business.*

Carol Shea, CEO, Olivetree Research
The clarity, directness, and simplicity of the ideas in this book work. Using the three tools in Plugged, *Krissi Barr is coaching me to transform my business from a traditional market research company into a world-class strategic brand intelligence agency.*

Scott Farmer, Chief Executive Officer, Cintas Corporation
Dan and Krissi weave important business lessons with golf to produce an original and amazingly impactful book. Plugged *will help everyone raise their game and improve the entire team's score. Its powerful principles are perfect for anyone and any team.*

P.B. Dye, world-famous golf course architect
Plugged *is a must-read for all golfers and for those who want to learn how to apply the lessons of golf to life and business.*

Doug Hall, author of *Jump Start Your Business Brain* (named one of the "100 Best Business Books of All Time")
A great one-two combination of market wisdom and winning ways from a great one-two team. The real-world insight described in Plugged *will benefit all readers.*

Dick Bere, Retired President, The Kroger Company and Chief Operating Officer, Crayons to Computers
Plugged *is an outstanding method of demonstrating principles of leadership and management. The plot of the story between AlphaMax and Trident certainly sets the stage for the 19th hole. It should be required reading for all managers.*

John West, Vice President Engineering, CSX Corporation
Plugged *is relevant on many fronts: teambuilding, leadership, personal challenge, and business adaptation. It's perfect for companies dealing with change. The characters, their issues, and thoughts drew me into the story. The writing was so clean it felt as smooth as an Augusta green.*

Chip Klosterman, President, Klosterman Baking Company
Not to brag, but I know a thing or two about making a lot of dough. Follow the recipe the Barrs have cooked up and you'll find yourself rolling in it, too.

Peter Davies, General Manager, The Wianno Club
The lessons in Plugged *will provide your business with a forward path that is essential in an uncertain economy. Dan and Krissi Barr's business strategy is the perfect model for country club and resort management—or for any business—to improve the bottom line and increase customer satisfaction.*

Jim Pancero, author of *You Can Always Sell More—How To Improve Any Sales Force* and President, Jim Pancero Inc. (an advanced sales training company)
Like few books before it, Plugged *demystifies the inner workings of business while taking the reader on an exhilarating ride. As a sales consultant, I found the lessons ring true and the situations real. Krissi and Dan's resulting blueprint for success can impact both your selling efforts and your life. Even though I'm still trying to finish a round of golf "shooting below my weight," I still loved this book!*

Crystal Faulkner, Founding Partner, Cooney, Faulkner & Stevens
I'll never forget the "ah ha!" moment when I read this book. The economy was in a tailspin, and while we had strong relationships with our customers, I knew that if we applied the lessons in Plugged, *we could help them weather the storm and be even more successful. Krissi showed us how to use the three tools in our company, for our customers...and we've never looked back.*

Introduction

Getting the right things done. Sounds really simple, doesn't it? But at a very early age, most of us were already experts at rationalizing not doing the right things. *I brushed my teeth yesterday! Why can't I do my homework after the movie? I promise I'll clean my room this weekend!*

Well, the experts have grown up and turned pro. *I'll turn in my status report tomorrow! Do I really need to visit that customer this month? I'm too busy to do strategic planning.* In today's topsy-turvy economic climate, companies everywhere are finding themselves in tough situations. When it happens to you—and it will—the question is *will you be able to pull your team together and overcome the challenges?*

There are inevitable bumps in the road ahead, both in business and in your personal life. This book is about three powerful tools that will help you shake off decades of bad habits and get the right things done. It's set against a backdrop of golf, arguably the most challenging sport in the world...after business, that is.

Each of these seemingly different worlds—business, life, and golf—has surprising commonality. Each is difficult, complicated, and can be rewarding. Each has its own set of rules, its own language, and its own scorecard. Most importantly, each of these realms has a similar path to excellence.

Everyone measures success differently. For you, maybe it's leading your company to growth and prosperity, or sending your children to college, or finally having the lowest score in your foursome. However you define it, this book is a road map for you and your team on how to dig out and get the right things done.

Foreword by Dr. Paul Hersey

In Lewis Carroll's *Alice in Wonderland*, Alice arrives at the intersection of many roads; looking up she sees the Cheshire cat smiling from the tree above.

She asks the cat, "Which road should I take?"

And he responds, "Where is it you'd like to go?"

Alice replies, "I really don't know."

The cat responds, "Then take any road."

Life will hand you an intersection of your own. It is the way of things. Will you know which road to take?

What follows is a parable. Look beneath the surface for what it means to you. This is a tale with a lesson worth learning. May it help guide you down the right road.

Enjoy . . .

Dr. Paul Hersey, Owner and Founder of the Center for Leadership Studies, "Home of Situational Leadership®." A world-renowned organizational development authority, Dr. Hersey has worked with Maslov and Drucker.

Teeing Up The Cast

Chet McGill—vice president of sales at AlphaMax

Reggie Ward—vice president of operations at Trident, Chet's biggest customer

Walter Murdock—president of AlphaMax

Carol Hayes—vice president of customer service at AlphaMax

Mike "Duke" Duchovny—vice president of production at AlphaMax

Felix Sanchez—works in shipping department at AlphaMax

Oscar Brabonskowitz—vice president of information technology at AlphaMax

Al Huff—operations supervisor at AlphaMax

Wayne Davidson—Chet's brother-in-law

"Doc" Lanier—golfing buddy

Lou—works at Meadowfield Golf Club

Jack—works at Meadowfield Golf Club

Grace McGill—Chet's wife

Burt Gregory—Meadowfield's head golf pro

 Chapter One

Chet McGill had never seen his boss look so in-decisive. "Seriously, Walt, don't worry," Chet said. "Everything's going to be fine. Go!"

Walter Murdock, president of AlphaMax Manufacturing, fidgeted in his chair. "But what if something happens and you need to reach me?" Walt said. He stood up from his desk and began pacing. "These cabins don't have Internet or TVs or phones…and there's definitely no cell phone cover-age out there. Unless I hitch a ride to the nearest town, I'll be totally out of communications!"

"And that's exactly what you promised Mrs. Murdock, isn't it?" replied Chet. "You've had this trip planned for months, and, to be honest, you could use the time off. Besides, it's only a week. I'll make sure nothing goes sideways." Chet looked at his watch. "Time to go or you'll miss the plane."

Walt took a deep breath, forced a smile, and grabbed his cell phone. "You're probably right; things will be fine. But remember, I'm leaving you in charge, so if something does happen, you make the decision."

Chet nodded. "Go and enjoy your vacation, and don't worry about AlphaMax. You can count on me. Everything's under control."

Chet McGill, vice president of sales at AlphaMax, looked like he had just been punched in the stomach. "Holy cow," he said. "Okay, hang on for a second while I put you on speaker." He pressed a button on his phone. "All right, Felix, I'm sitting here with Carol Hayes, our VP of customer service. Carol, I've got Felix Sanchez on the phone. He just dropped off a delivery at Trident and...Felix, tell Carol what you heard."

"Like I said, it's not my fault," Felix said. "I was delivering a shipment to Trident, and one of my buddies on the loading dock said our competitor had just taken a tour of their facility. He said it looked like Trident was thinking about switching to them."

Chet looked at his suddenly panicked co-worker. "Have you heard anything about this?"

Carol shook her head. "No, but we mostly deal

with their order entry and billing departments, so we're not in that loop." Carol leaned closer to the speakerphone. "Felix, was that the delivery of back-ordered parts that you just dropped off?"

"That's the one," he replied. "They were supposed to be there yesterday, but the production department didn't have them ready by noon—which is our cut-off for shipments—so we scheduled them for delivery today."

"But I heard that order was ready at eleven," Carol said. "Why wasn't it delivered yesterday?"

"Department policy," Felix explained, "is to ship everything that's ready by noon, but the paperwork on the Trident order wasn't approved until after lunch. That's just how we do it." Felix paused, then

added, "Look, I don't set the rules, but I know our supervisor was in a big department meeting all morning, so we just got a bad break on the timing."

Chet felt like snapping the pencil in his hand. "Did you hear anything else that might be important?"

"Well, my buddy told me all of the big honchos at Trident were involved in the red carpet tour...even the ones that needed directions to the receiving department."

Chet stared at the phone. "Okay, thanks for the call, and let me know if you hear anything else." He hung up and turned to Carol. "Looks like we picked a bad time to screw up that order."

Friday, 5:25 P.M., AlphaMax Manufacturing

Chet pored over the most recent financial report, not really sure what he was even looking for. *Last quarter's sales look pretty normal,* he thought. *Orders are off, but that's typical this time of year.* Nothing in the data jumped out as a red flag. But in his gut he knew somthing was wrong.

 **Chapter Two**

"What's up, Lou?" Chet asked as he zipped past the club's starter toward the three men standing at the first tee. Chet slammed on the brakes and skidded his golf cart to a stop on the wet pavement. As usual, he was late for his regular weekend game.

"Hey, Mario Andretti, you're up," said Wayne Davidson, Chet's brother-in-law. "And, yes, we're all three hundred yards down the middle of the fairway."

Chet hurriedly began changing his shoes. "Sorry I'm late, but the traffic getting here was ridiculous! We get a little rain overnight and people drive like it was a foot of snow."

The group's eldest member, dentist "Doc" Lanier, slid his glasses down his nose and looked at Chet. "Funny, it wasn't so bad an hour ago."

"Hey, back off my partner," said Mike "Duke" Duchovny as he strapped his bag to the back of Chet's cart. "Anyone can break a hundred when they're warmed up, but it takes real skill to do it when you're stiff, rushed, and angry!"

Chet yanked his driver from the bag and hustled to the tee box. "If I get off to a slow start at least I can blame it on not warming up," he said as he rooted through his pockets. "Hey, Duke, toss me a tee."

Duke—who worked at AlphaMax—flicked a

tee to Chet. "Man, I hope you at least brought some cash," he said, "because I've got a bad feeling about today's game."

Chet teed up his ball and took a couple of practice swings. *Tee it high and let it fly*, he said to himself as he addressed the ball. He swung furiously, sending the ball high into the air and two hundred and forty-five yards down the right side of the fairway.

"It's like I always say, Chet drives for show, then putts three or four times, and the world is in equilibrium," Wayne said as he climbed into his cart.

"Laugh now, boys, but I've got a secret weapon today," Chet said, sliding his driver back in the bag. "Check out this baby, the Moonwalker 3000."

Chet pulled out a futuristic-looking club with curved titanium counterweights and fancy markings. "This is the ultimate quick-fix—the hottest putter on the tour and guaranteed to take five strokes off my game *instantly*."

"The only guarantee is you had to take out a second mortgage to buy that thing," Doc said.

As they drove up the cart path to the balls, Duke and Chet talked about work. "Yeah, sales are holding up so far, but last month's orders were down," Chet said. "Things are starting to slip with the overall slowdown in the economy, and now I've got a new problem to worry about."

Duke gazed with curiosity at Chet.

"You know Reggie Ward from Trident?" Chet asked.

"Sure," Duke said. "You're playing with him in the Member-Guest tournament next weekend, aren't you?"

"Yeah, lucky me." Chet slowed the cart as they crested a hill. "I'm sure your production team has cranked out enough Trident-logoed parts to notice that they're our biggest customer."

Duke nodded.

"I just found out they're thinking about switching to another company," Chet said. "If we lose Trident, I'm sunk."

"We're *all* sunk," Duke said as they rounded a bend in the cart path. "We can't afford to lose our number one account...especially in this economy."

"Tell me about it," Chet said. "I've got a good relationship with Reggie, but this new competitor is apparently telling Trident they can do the same things we do, only for a lot less, and the procurement folks are buying it." Chet took off his golf hat and ran a hand through his hair. "Shipping didn't get that back order to them until yesterday, and now we may have to drop our prices just to hang on to their business...that is *if* we can hang on to their business."

Chet stopped the cart. "I don't know if there's much else we can do...the competition is just cheaper than we are," he said. "To top it all off, the only thing Reggie likes more than winning is driving a hard bargain."

Both men smiled uncomfortably. "Try to forget about that for now," Duke said.

Chet nodded and hopped out of the cart. As he approached his ball he let out a groan. "Oh, great... my ball is plugged." He'd hit the ball so high that when it landed, it became buried in the wet grass and mud. "What's the ruling on this?"

"You can pull your ball out of the muck, clean it off, and drop it," Duke said. "The ball just can't end up closer to the hole. So while it looks like a bad situation, you actually get another chance, and there's no penalty."

"One shot into the round and I already need a break," Chet said as he wiped the mud off his ball, dropped it on the wet grass, and began eyeing his next shot.

Duke smiled. "Let's see you knock your ball on the green so we can find out how that newfangled putter of yours really works."

With a six iron in hand, Chet put a smooth swing on the ball and knocked it pin high and twenty-five feet to the left of the cup. *"That's* what I'm talking about!" he said.

By the time all four golfers were on the green the sun had finally burst through the clouds. Chet strode confidently through the wet, bent grass with his Moonwalker 3000 in hand. "Looks like I'm away," he said as he quickly eyed his putt.

"I can't wait to see what a three-hundred-dollar putter does in the hands of a twenty-five-handicap golfer," said Wayne.

Chet hovered over his ball for a moment and said, "I'll have you know my handicap's down to an eighteen." He drew back the putter and rapped the ball, which ran downhill, picked up speed, broke left, and raced ten feet past the hole. "Aw, come on, the green looked slow!"

"I hope you left the price tag on," said Doc. "It makes it easier to return."

Saturday, 1:50 P.M., 18th Green, Meadowfield Golf Club

"Come on, partner, sink this putt and redeem yourself," said Duke. "And save us from losing another five bucks."

Chet had been striking the ball well all day, but

his putting problems continued. He needed to roll in a five-footer for bogie and a round of ninety-six.

Duke stood behind him, helping size up the shot. "Breaks a little right, not much," he said.

Chet nodded, took a quick practice stroke, and approached the ball. He pulled back the new putter and gently accelerated, giving the ball a gentle tap. It rolled softly toward the left edge, caught the lip, spun around the back of the cup, and came to rest an inch from the hole.

Chet shook his head in disbelief. "This new putter stinks," he said quietly.

"That one's good by me," snickered Wayne as he reached out to shake Duke's hand. "Always a profit, um, I mean, *pleasure* playing with you guys."

 ## Chapter Three

Chet was thoroughly annoyed. He'd lost twenty bucks, shot a ninety-seven, and spoiled a perfectly lovely day for golf. Most aggravating, his expensive new club hadn't improved his putting a bit. After saying goodbye to his pals, he paused outside the pro shop and glanced over at the practice green. *A couple of practice putts and I'll have my new putter mastered*, he thought.

He was still brooding about the Moonwalker 3000 as he dropped his ball on the green, aimed at the nearest cup, and gave it a poke. Too short. He decided to put a little more oomph on the next one, and his second putt was a little long. His eighteen-inch come-backer rimmed out.

"Aw, come on!" he exclaimed a little louder than golf etiquette allows.

He took dead aim at the practice cup fifty feet away, brow furrowed. *Give it a chance, make sure it gets to the hole.* He took a long backswing and gave it a whack. The ball shot away, buzzed past the hole, and headed off the green. It finally came to a stop mercifully hidden in the long grass, as if it, too, were embarrassed.

Chet stood a moment, with a look of total bewilderment on his face. He glanced from the Moonwalker 3000 to the ball seventy feet away, then back to the club. He glanced around the practice green to see if anyone had been watching the lousy putt, but he was alone in his misery.

As he stood motionless, several thoughts raced through his mind. *Should I break this club over my knee? Yell a profanity at the top of my lungs? Quit golf?*

Against every urge in his body, he decided to retrieve his ball. "I hear stamp collecting is a lot of fun," he muttered, walking head down toward his ball. "I could start with the fat Elvis stamp, then collect ones from the national parks I've been to…"

As Chet reached to pick up his ball, he saw a glint of something out of the corner of his eye, near the trees twenty yards away. He walked closer, reached down, and picked it up. It was a putter, half-buried in the grass. The club had an ancient-looking wooden shaft, tattered leather grip, and no indication who owned it. In fact, its only markings were three small indentations on the top of the club head and a pealing sticker on the shaft that said "PAR."

I'll take this as a sign from the golf gods that my work here is done, he thought. He gathered his things and headed toward Lou, the club's starter, with the old putter in hand.

Lou was an energetic man in his seventies who for the last decade had greeted players, explained the local rules, told the same jokes, and helped foursomes get off the first tee on time. He was the smiling face of Meadowfield Golf Club, a true golf aficionado who felt retirement was more fun when he came to work every day.

"Hey, Lou, check out what I found in the weeds over by the practice green," Chet said, handing over the putter he'd found. "Looks like it's been there for years."

Lou's quizzical look turned into a broad smile as he examined the club. "Well, I'll be, a Par putter! I had one like this when I was a boy. Best putter I ever had! They just don't make 'em like this anymore."

"Probably because no one would buy them," Chet said.

"It's because no one would pay a couple hundred bucks for anything this simple," replied Lou. "With one of these, it's back to the basics." Lou pointed to the markings on the putter. "Before every putt I used to look at these three lines on the top of the club to remind me of the three most important fundamentals in putting, the—"

"Wait, let me guess," Chet interrupted. "Distance to the hole, break, and slope of the green…you know, is it uphill or downhill? *At least those putting lessons I took weren't a total waste,* Chet thought.

"Exactly right," Lou said. "Just don't forget about the speed of the green and your grip and stance. But as long as you take time before every putt to concentrate on what the three lines represent and then *visualize* the ball going in the hole, you'll do all right."

Chet feigned interest. "Hmmm. Three lines… what a concept. Any idea who lost it?"

Lou shook his head. "I checked the message board this morning. We got some folks looking for drivers and wedges, the usual stuff, but no one's said anything about losing one of these."

"Hard to imagine the owner wouldn't miss this baby," Chet said sarcastically as he headed toward the clubhouse. "Now that I have my new Moonwalker 3000, all my putting problems are behind me, so if you want to keep it, it's all yours. Or take it to the next *Antiques Roadshow* to see what it's worth."

"How'd you putt today?" Lou asked with a slight smile.

Chet stopped and looked back, shuffling his feet uncomfortably. "Um, not so good. This new putter was cold as ice. But once I get used to it I—"

"Do me a favor," Lou said, walking toward Chet. "Keep this old putter until someone asks for it. I think sometimes the Lost and Found is more *lost* than *found*." He handed the club to Chet. "This way, if someone does post for it, I'll know where it is."

Chet took the putter, looking at it doubtfully, like a teenage boy who just received an ugly sweater as a birthday gift from his great aunt.

"Besides," continued Lou, "you might actually want to give this old putter a try. Sometimes you have to go back to the basics."

Chet laughed. "Okay, okay, I'll give it a nice temporary home here in the Land of Misfit Toys." He slid the putter into his bag and headed to his locker.

Saturday, 3:30 P.M., Old Stable Road

As Chet drove home he thought about his two "new" putters. He hated to admit it, but the Moonwalker 3000 was a disappointment. He bolstered his spirits with the thought that he had a week to get more comfortable with it before the big tournament.

He smiled remembering how Lou had made him hold on to the club he found. *That old putter was such a piece of junk. No wonder it had been abandoned. Probably thrown away for good reason.*

When he stopped for a red light, he reached

for his cell phone and dialed his biggest customer. He breathed a sigh of relief when it went straight to voice mail.

"Hey, Reggie. Chet McGill. Just wanted to confirm that we're still on for a tune-up round tomorrow at ten. This is our year to win the Member-Guest, and I'm feeling the mojo! See you in the morning."

Chet ended the call and turned the corner, suddenly deep in thought. *The economy is up and down, orders are off, and our biggest client is shopping us.* Chet drove slowly through his neighborhood, working his way toward home. *Plus Walt is out of communications on vacation and he left me in charge. And I can't putt my way out of a paper bag.*

He turned into his driveway and put the car in park. *Nice to see my house is still here. Everything else in my world seems to be on fire.*

 ## Chapter Four

Chet brimmed with optimism as he walked through
Meadowfield's modest clubhouse, down the stairs to
the men's locker room, and over to the third aisle.
He opened locker 102's beige metal door, sat down,
and hurriedly began putting on his golf shoes.
*Today's the day my new putter finally turns things
around*, he thought as he laced up his spikes. He
stood and was ready to close the locker door when
he noticed a three-by-five card with a handwritten
note beside his rain vest. It read:

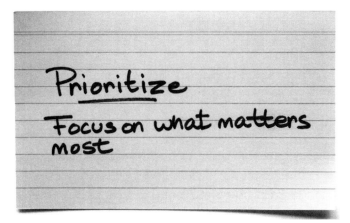

Unfamiliar handwriting, no signature, no indication
who wrote it. He looked around to see if someone
was about to claim authorship. No one.

How bizarre, he thought. *Now I'm getting cryptic,*

inspirational messages from a secret admirer. He closed his locker and headed out, still puzzled by the strange message. *Well, at least my pen pal didn't steal anything.*

He walked into the morning sun and saw Reggie Ward, the vice president of operations for Trident. Reggie was a local business legend who still carried the sturdy build of a former football player.

"Hey, Reggie," Chet said, shaking his hand firmly. "Beautiful day for golf."

"A lot nicer than that monsoon we played in last year," Reggie said. "Want to hit some balls or putt a little, or are you ready to go, as usual?"

"I vote for 'as usual,'" Chet replied. "Let's let Lou know we're here, load up a cart, and make some golf history."

There was a twosome ahead of them on the first tee, and as they waited they swung their drivers and talked.

"You should know that your competitor made a good impression with our director of purchasing," Reggie said soberly. "They toured our facility and now they're saying they can save us a lot of money while keeping service and quality high."

Chet nodded. "I heard they were trying to get in." He looked down at his feet, then up to Reggie. "You guys aren't looking at them seriously, are you?"

Just as intently, Reggie looked him in the eye. "We have to. Our margins are getting squeezed.

Everyone's scrambling to find ways to cut costs."
Reggie fiddled with the grip on his driver. "Costs are
rising, the economy is brutal, customers want lower
prices, and our employees still expect raises. We
need AlphaMax to step up and show us how you
can help make us more competitive."

"I want to make sure I understand something,"
Chet said. "When you say 'help make us more competitive,' what does that mean to you?"

Reggie took a half swing with his club as he
gathered his thoughts. "Well, price and total cost are
always in the equation, but quality, service, breadth
of product line, delivery times…all of those are critical. It's really pretty simple: we need to know we're
getting the very best overall value."

Chet nodded. He wanted to blurt out how the
competitor was losing key employees like rats off a
sinking ship, looked like they were going to lose a
major lawsuit, and had the industry's worst reputa-
tion for over-promising and under-delivering. Instead
he said, "We've been a great partner with Trident
for many years, and we've always come through for
you. When you look closely at the two of us, you'll
know we're the right choice. All I ask is that we get
the chance to make our case for why you should
stay with us."

"Fair enough," said Reggie. "You've earned that."

Then Lou called out, "Mr. McGill, if you're ready,
you and Mr. Ward have the tee."

"We're good," Chet called to Lou. Then he looked at Reggie and said, "We *are* good, aren't we?"

"Yeah, we're good," said Reggie with a grin. "Now let's see how much work we'll have to do to win the tournament."

Chet was relieved to see his partner smile, but he knew there was more beneath the surface. His biggest customer, Trident, was in jeopardy.

Switching into golf mode, Chet said, "I can't wait to show you my new one-putt wonder, the Moonwalker 3000. This baby's going to help us win it all!"

"In that case I say you tee it up and let's see what you got."

Sunday, 11:55 A.M., 9th Green, Meadowfield Golf Club

"Looks like it's your turn," said Reggie as he walked around the green to get a read on which way the ball would break. "Time for that that 'moon' thing of yours to get hot."

One small putt for me, Chet mused, *one giant leap for my self esteem.* He eyed the eight-foot putt, fiddled with his stance, and sent the ball rolling.

Short by ten inches.

His frustrated glare bored new dimples in his ball. He took three brisk steps and tapped it in. "Seven." *I just shot a fifty on the front nine when I ought to shoot a forty-one,* he thought. *Why the heck did I buy this stupid putter!*

Reggie didn't look at his partner. Instead, he crouched down to see in his mind's eye the way his six-foot putt would break. Once he saw it, he righted himself, took a practice stroke, addressed the ball, and drained it.

"Nice putt," said Chet, happy to be able to focus on something positive. "What's that give you, a forty-two for the front nine?"

Reggie plucked his ball from the cup. "Yeah. Hope I can keep it up on the back."

Chet nodded encouragingly as he put the flagstick back in the hole. As they walked off the green, Reggie put his arm on Chet's shoulder. "You've got nine more holes to show that putter who's the boss, so just stay confident," Reggie said. "You can do it."

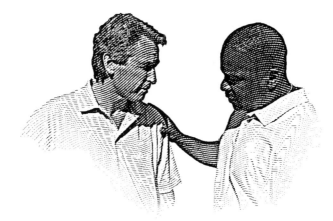

Chet's lips twisted into a forced smile. He wanted to believe he would find his putting stroke in the next two hours, but he certainly wasn't confident he would. "I'll give it my best," he said. "Maybe a hot dog at the turn will do the trick. Come to think of it, maybe what I need is a beer or two."

Sunday, 2:10 P.M., 18th Green, Meadowfield Golf Club

Chet wanted to quit. His front-nine woes had turned into a back-nine tailspin. Worse yet, it was all in full view of his biggest customer...perhaps his biggest *former* customer.

The blue skies and lush fairways provided a beautiful backdrop for an ugly final nine. Chet reluctantly reviewed his scorecard: one four, two fives, three sixes, a seven, and an eight. His ball striking had been good, but his short game—especially his putting—had been atrocious. Thankfully, they were on the final green, where he needed a six-foot putt to card his only par of the day.

"Looks pretty straight, maybe breaking an inch left at the end," Chet said, half to himself and half hoping for confirmation from Reggie. He stood over the ball and looked down the shaft of his putter. The Moonwalker 3000's gleaming clubface was supposed to give him confidence. It didn't. His stomach registered the same uncertainty he had felt hole after hole, putt after putt.

Come on, he thought. *This one's make-able, so make it!* He stroked the ball and watched as it rolled toward the right edge of the cup, finally coming to rest an inch away.

Gritting his teeth, he picked up his ball. "Five," he said, walking dejectedly behind Reggie, who placed his ball in front of his marker and began to study his shot.

"I need this for an eighty-five," Reggie said, as he approached his three-footer. "Hit it firm, take out the break," he said. He steadied his stocky frame, took a practice stroke, and knocked the ball into the back of the cup.

"Great round, Reggie!" Chet said as he shook his partner's hand. "I guess I'm saving my clutch putts for the tournament."

"You played well until you got on the green," Reggie said. "Just figure out how to get that blade working, and we can win it next Saturday."

Easier said than done, thought Chet. The shiny Moonwalker 3000 clattered against the old putter as Chet shoved it into the bag. He climbed into the driver's seat and drove toward the pro shop, giving a wry look to Reggie as he said, "Unless my new putter starts living up to its billing, I'm going to have to actually work at this game."

Sunday, 2:25 P.M., Locker 102, Meadowfield Golf Club

Alone again, Chet plunked down on the bench in front of his locker and began taking off his spikes. He had shot one of the worst rounds of golf in the last two years—one hundred and one. To make matters worse, he was temporarily in charge of the company, and now their biggest customer was hanging by a thread. *What a day*, he thought. As he opened his locker to change into his street shoes, he read the perplexing note card once more:

Prioritize
Focus on what matters most

As he thought about the message it dawned on him that someone was trying to help him. But who? And why?

 Chapter Five

Chet looked at his watch as Mike Duchovny, vice president of production, strolled into the room. "Nice of you to join us, Duke," Chet said. "I thought emergency meetings were supposed to start on time."

"The clock on the coffee machine must be off," Duke shot back as he plopped into a seat. Carol Hayes, vice president of customer service, gave Chet an uncomfortable glance.

Duke leaned back in his chair. "So we're here to talk about how Walter goes on vacation and we get this Trident mess dumped in our laps, right?"

"Let's stay positive," Chet said in a tone that belied his words. Addressing the group he said, "I spoke with Reggie Ward yesterday, and he confirmed the rumor that Trident is looking at the competition. I know *we* think we're doing a great job, but Trident's purchasing team is trying to cut costs and make sure they're getting the best value. We need to come up with a game plan to save the account, so let's roll up our sleeves and get on it."

The group murmured in agreement.

"Duke," Chet started, "what can your manufacturing team do to help the situation?"

"First of all, we're not the problem here," Duke said. "The shipping department screwed up that order. Plus, I hear the competition uses inferior-quality parts and just cranks out the junk. They lie about what they can do, and they over-promise and under-deliver, so I don't think we should even—"

"Whoa, hang on a second," Chet interrupted. "I'm just trying to fill in while Walt's gone and get an understanding of where we are in this situation, not lay the blame on you or anyone else. So how much cost can you take out of the production process?"

Duke frowned and looked down as he shook his head. "We're a lean, mean, manufacturing machine. The less-time-sensitive parts are made overseas, and the rest of the parts are made here in our plant that we run 24/7." Duke flipped through some reports and looked up. "Unless you want to cut back on quality or have longer delivery times, this is all we can do."

Chet looked directly at Duke. "I hear you, but now's the time to find some new ways to remove cost. Or maybe get some samples from the competitor and do a side-by-side comparison to prove our quality difference." Chet paused a moment as he racked his brain for other ideas. "Here's another thought: let's dig into Trident's manufacturing and distribution processes so we can come up with some plans for joint savings."

"All good ideas for sure, but don't forget your sales team is always making promises that my production team gets stuck with, so look at your group, too," Duke said. "Besides, I think Trident may be bluffing—just trying to get us to give them more."

Chet shook his head. "This isn't Trident and the sales team both blowing smoke. We've got a real problem, and I need you to look at this from every angle and see what you can do to move us in the right direction."

Duke shrugged and said, "Okay."

Chet grimaced and made a note, then said, "Carol?"

Carol Hayes was AlphaMax's newest vice president. Her customer service team had formerly been part of the sales group but had recently split off to put more focus on serving customer needs.

"We have a service manager and two service coordinators that spend most of their time on Trident," she said. "Our customer satisfaction rating with Trident is better than it's been in years, and we just rolled out our interface with the new electronic billing system that Trident implemented." Carol looked uneasy. "That project was three months behind schedule, but it's now up and running smoothly. And it cost us thirty-five thousand dollars more than we thought it would, which didn't make Walt very happy."

"Back to the customer satisfaction for a minute," Chet said. "So how happy are they with us now?"

"Trident's customer satisfaction score would be a lot higher if they didn't keep changing their orders on us," Carol said as she rifled through her notes.

Finding the paper she wanted, she said, "It says we're up to an eighty-two out of a hundred, which is pretty good."

"As I recall that's a B minus in high school," Chet replied, "and as my mom used to say, that isn't good enough. We can do better!"

As Chet considered their next steps, the words on the note card from his golf locker leapt to mind. *Prioritize: Focus on what matters most.* Chet looked at the long faces of the managers in the room. *This crisis is bigger than my putting problems,* he thought. *Why not give it a try?*

"Okay, here's the plan," he said. "Let's just focus on what matters most and go back to the basics. Duke, take another look at fine-tuning the mix of offshore and domestic production to see if there's anything we could produce more efficiently. And base it on their forecasts, not historical sales. Also, why don't you spend tomorrow with Trident's production planning group so we're sure we know what they *really* want, and see if there are any new ideas we can come up with."

"Good plan," Duke said, "but I've got my monthly staff meeting tomorrow and my status report is due Wednesday. Why don't I just email their production planning group to see if they have any feedback for us?"

Chet stared at him, dumbfounded. "Are you serious? None of that other stuff matters! You need to meet with them face to face. *Tomorrow.*"

Duke looked away. "Okay. But they usually can't meet on such short notice."

Chet looked straight at Duke. "I don't care if you have to camp out in their parking lot. Get in there to see them!"

Chet tried to get his blood pressure back under control as he turned his attention to Carol. "I need you to find some new ways we can get closer to the customer. You know, find out how we can make it easier for them to order or find ways to get their products to market faster. And, yes, that means I want you to meet with them tomorrow, too."

Carol nodded in agreement.

Chet walked to the window and looked out at the nearby oak trees swaying in the light summer breeze. "Also, Carol, let's put together a list of the times your team went the extra mile…the times you stayed late and worked weekends to make sure Trident got their orders on time. Let's build the case for upgrading that B minus to an A."

Carol nodded again while scribbling a note to herself.

Chet turned to face his associates. "AlphaMax has been a great partner with Trident for years, and now's our chance to show them what we're going to do differently to deliver even better performance and make them more competitive."

Duke bobbed his head. "As long as we're all

here," he said, "I wanted to talk about the new advertising mock-ups that marketing sent over and—"

"Right now it's all Trident, all the time," Chet interrupted. "In fact, let's get the entire company focused on Trident. If we don't hold on to their business, nothing else matters." Chet stood up and pushed in his chair. "All right, we've got a lot to do. Let's get to work."

 Chapter Six

"You got it," Chet said. "Now let's just make sure we get that shipping policy updated ASAP. Thanks." Hanging up the phone, he returned to his notes.

- *The Perfect Storm:* Walt is gone and I'm in charge; the economy is in the tank; our competition is going after our biggest customer.

- *Top priority:* Hold on to Trident's business.

- *Reasons why we're in this situation:* We became complacent and comfortable. Success malaise.

- *What we can do now:* Come up with new ways to work with Trident; upgrade their perception of us; get more efficient.

- *Gather data:* Confirm product defect rate and service complaint resolution status in the last year. Talk with our partners. Quantify investments we made in new equipment and software for Trident and how they have paid off from the customer's point of view.

- *Focus:* Make sure everyone knows what success looks like, and get the team totally focused on achieving it.

He called home and left a message for Grace, his wife. "Hi, honey. This is going to be a crazy week.

I need to get some things done before I leave the office tonight, so if you could just leave me some leftovers in the fridge that would be perfect."

Perfect? Chet thought as he hung up. *No, perfect would be a steak dinner to celebrate holding on to Trident's business, but tonight, cold meatloaf will have to do.*

 ## Chapter Seven

"So, that's our situation," Chet said at the end of his opening comments. "One last thing: I know you're all working hard, but more than ever we need to work hard on the *right* things. Now let's open up the discussion. I'm really looking for your comments and suggestions on how we can win this one."

The crowd of office and manufacturing department employees remained silent for a moment, letting it all sink in. Finally, someone spoke up.

"Mr. McGill, about the—"

"Call me Chet, eh...Jason," Chet said, smiling as he leaned over to read the name on the man's shirt.

"Okay, Chet," the man replied, to a twitter of chuckles from the others. "If we don't retain Trident's business, what's gonna happen to our people on the shop floor or in the office?"

Chet paused a moment before answering. "Let me first say that I'm confident that we are going to hold on to Trident's business. But if for some reason we don't, it isn't going to be pretty...for *any* of us. The government isn't going to bail us out. We're all in this together. We're all members of the AlphaMax team, and that's why I'm talking to you and asking for your recommendations on how we can hold on to their business."

Pulling out a pad of paper and a pen, Chet added, "I'm all ears."

When he left the meeting thirty minutes later, he had six pages of suggestions, ideas, and comments. *Time to roll up my sleeves*, he thought.

Tuesday, 7:20 P.M., Meadowfield Golf Club

An hour's worth of sun remained as Chet passed through the door of Meadowfield's men's locker room. He had spent the rest of the day working on Trident, but he knew he needed to practice his putting before he went home.

The Member-Guest Tournament was Saturday, and somehow he felt if he played well it would help his case with Trident. *Reggie wants to win, so now's not the time to look weak*, he thought.

He paused as he sat down in front of his locker. Would there be another note? He opened the locker with a mixture of curiosity and trepidation.

There it was.

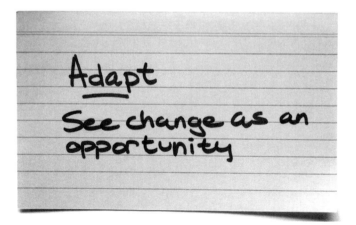

The message struck a chord and he sat pondering it for a long moment. *How do I need to adapt? What changes do I need to make?* He thought about his weak putting and how he had purchased a new putter to change it. *Wasn't that enough?*

He put the note on top of the previous card, changed into his spikes, and headed out of the locker room to get his golf bag.

"Hello, Mr. McGill. Are you going to try to squeeze in nine tonight?" It was Jack, the friendly, sandy-haired young man who managed the bag storage area.

"Not tonight," Chet said with a chuckle. "I know this is hard to believe, but I'm going to practice my putting. Got to plug some holes in my game before the Member-Guest."

"Sounds like a good idea," Jack said as he turned to get the bag. "I mean, not that you need the practice, sir, that's not what I meant to…." Jack's voice trailed off as he disappeared into the storage room.

Chet had to laugh. When Jack returned with his bag, Chet grabbed it, slung the strap over his shoulder, and handed Jack a five-dollar bill. "Just don't tell anyone I was practicing. Wouldn't want the oddsmakers in Vegas to know about this."

"Thanks," Jack said. "And your secret's safe with me."

Chet walked the short distance to the empty practice green and set his bag next to it. He fished out a pair of balls and tossed them toward one of the holes. Reaching for the Moonwalker 3000, he thought about the two note cards.

The words suddenly registered, and Chet realized that what mattered most was better putting and that he needed to make some changes.

He gave the vacant practice area a once-over, then declared to his invisible advisor, "Okay, I get it! I'll make a change." He reached into his bag, bypassing the Moonwalker 3000, and pulled out the battered old putter. "See? I'm giving this one a try, too." He knew an observer might think he'd lost his mind, talking to himself that way, but he no longer cared.

He walked to his first ball and took a practice stroke. The old putter felt good in his hands. As he placed the club behind the ball he noticed the three lines and backed off.

He thought, *Why not give Lou's idea a chance? Three lines: distance, break, and slope...then visualize it going in the hole.*

He stood back and estimated the distance, judged the slight break, assessed the uphill slope, and paused to visualize the ball going in the hole. Then he addressed the ball and gave it a stroke. The ball rolled swiftly off the face, slowed as it went up the slight incline, curved as it caught the edge of an undulation, and died in the hole. The sweet sound of the ball rattling to a stop brought the first wholehearted smile to his face in days.

"*That's* what I'm talking about," Chet said quietly. He approached his second ball on the green and took aim at the same hole. "Let's see if lightning can strike twice." He considered the three lines, assessed the green, hit the ball, and watched as it, too, went in.

Chet stood motionless for a moment. He couldn't remember the last time he had made two consecutive putts, let alone two long ones. He shook himself back into the here and now with new determination and confidence.

He retrieved the balls from the cup and tossed them cavalierly into the center of the green. Approaching the first ball, he took sight of a practice cup less than a dozen feet away.

Distance, break, slope...then visualize, he thought. He readied himself, struck the ball, and followed it as it came up a whisker short, with half the ball hanging over the front of the hole. *Not bad. Next time a little firmer.*

He repeated the mantra, followed each step, and hit the second ball. It rolled toward the cup, curved around the back, and plopped in the hole.

"Coming in the back door!" he exclaimed.

Eager to do it again, he grabbed the two balls and looked for the next hole to victimize. *Go big or go home*, he said to himself. He set his sights on the farthest cup at the edge of the practice green. Again he went through the steps: *Forty feet away, should break three feet right, slightly downhill, visualize the putt going in.*

He settled in over the ball and confidently swung the old putter. The ball took off down the hill, broke right, and came to rest a foot from the hole. *Learn from that and try to get inside the first one.* After reanalyzing the shot, Chet putted the second ball and watched as it finally curled to a stop just behind the cup, leaving only a tap in.

For the next twenty minutes he continued his practice with amazing results. Uphill putts, downhill putts, short ones, long ones, big breaks, no breaks: all with the same astounding results.

So this is what it feels like to be in the zone, he thought. *I could get used to this.*

With darkness approaching, he finally packed up and headed over to see Jack.

"How'd it go?" asked Jack, taking the bag.

Chet rested his arm on the counter and said, "You ever have one of those days when everything goes in?"

Jack smiled and said, "Just a few. It's a pretty awesome feeling, isn't it?"

"Honestly, I've never had that experience before. It was surreal. I could hardly miss." Chet smiled and handed Jack a ten-dollar bill. "Here, maybe the key is being a big tipper." Chet looked around to see if anyone was within earshot. "This isn't a dream, is it? We *are* having this conversation, right?"

"If this were a dream," Jack replied, "you'd be handing me a hundred-dollar bill."

Chet laughed and waved goodbye. "One more thing," he said turning back. "Has anyone asked about that ratty old putter I found a few days ago?"

Jack shook his head. "No, sir, but I check the message board every day, so I'll let you know if anything comes up."

 *Chapter Eight*

Trident. All Chet could think about was Trident. The contract represented 20 percent of AlphaMax's sales, and if they lost their largest customer, jobs would be lost, a year would be spent in the red, and there sure wouldn't be any bonuses. Chet couldn't let that happen…especially while Walt was out of contact.

He was deep in thought when the phone rang. It was Reggie Ward.

"I'm just checking on a couple of outstanding issues," Reggie said. "How are things progressing on your end?"

"If you'd asked me that question a few days ago, I would have had a different answer," Chet responded. "But today things are great. I've got the entire AlphaMax team focused on finding ways to bring more value to Trident, and we've come up with some terrific ideas."

"Glad to hear it."

"And on a personal athletic note," Chet continued, "I was practicing my putting last night, and I am happy to report that I think I've found my stroke. I switched over to an old putter I found, and it's like magic."

"Winners find a way to win, so I know you'll come through in the clutch," Reggie said. "Back to business, though. Our purchasing team has your competitor coming in for a presentation Friday morning. I have to tell you they've made a very good impression on us so far. Anyway, I'd like AlphaMax to come in Friday at two o'clock for your turn. Can you guys be ready by then?"

"I usually get a pedicure and foot massage on Friday afternoons, but I'll see if I can move some things around," Chet joked. "Two o'clock sounds good. I'm looking forward to showing you why AlphaMax is the right partner for Trident. See you Friday."

After hanging up, Chet called his team to let them know about the meeting. Then he sat back and let Reggie's words sink in: "Winners find a way to win, so I know you'll come through in the clutch."

Talk about pressure.

Wednesday, 10:00 A.M., AlphaMax Manufacturing

"So here's the deal," Chet said to the management team assembled in the big conference room. "Our meeting with Trident is at two o'clock on Friday. That gives us a little over two days to finalize the biggest presentation in AlphaMax's history. I know we're getting together tomorrow morning, but I wanted to touch base now so we're all on the same page."

As he looked around the room he saw Duke checking his BlackBerry. "Do you have some late-breaking news on Trident?" Chet asked.

Without looking up Duke replied, "No, just saving the world one email at a time."

Chet nearly exploded. "Everyone: cell phones off! Not vibrate, not silent, not Morse code but *off*!" He continued as people reached for their phones to comply. "This isn't business as usual, people. We need to band together and focus 100 percent of our attention on keeping Trident. So unless our building catches fire or someone stops breathing, nothing is more important than whatever you're doing to help keep Trident. Nothing!"

The team sat in stunned silence.

"This is our moment of truth," Chet said, lowering his intensity. "We have a rare opportunity to show our biggest customer—and ourselves—what we're made of. Excuse the melodrama, but we will either rise to the occasion or be blinded by these distractions and fail."

After a pause, a hand went up. "I know you're just our temporary president this week, but I have to say that in my fifteen years at AlphaMax, this isn't how we've ever done things." It was Al Huff, an operations supervisor. "We've always approached our problems methodically and set up committees to analyze them. I know you're trying, but you've thrown everyone into a complete frenzy over Trident. This isn't how Walt runs the company."

Chet fiddled with his pen for a moment before he replied. "Thanks for that feedback, Al. I'm sure there are others who are thinking the same thing. As I was listening to your comments I was reminded of my all-time favorite line from a movie. It was in *Star Wars* when Yoda said 'Do or do not. There is no try.' Now is not the time for me or any of us to *try* to save Trident; it's the time to *do* it."

Chet paused as he picked up his notes. "Feel free to write a memo to Walt on my management style or lack thereof, but for now let's quickly review where we are and the status of each of your assignments. Oh, and one more thing: I'm not asking each of you to turn your world upside-down just for the heck of it. We need to rethink how we work with Trident—and our other customers—and then be willing to make the difficult but necessary changes to better meet their needs.

"For example, let's re-examine any process or procedure we haven't updated in the last five years. Take a brutally honest look at whether your department's objectives trump the goals of the company. Ask yourself if everything you do brings the kind of value customers like Trident find meaningful."

Chet slowly looked at the shell-shocked faces around the room. "I've made the personal commitment to embrace whatever changes we need to make, and I really need each of you to do the same. Okay, let's go around the table and get an update on where things stand."

After the meeting ended, Chet approached Duke.

"I want to apologize for calling you out like that in front of everyone," Chet said. "I should have done that in private."

Duke shook his head. "You needed to send that message. Not just to me but to the entire team. I get it now. No more excuses...just get it done." Duke stood up and grabbed his phone. "Now if you'll pardon me, I've got a follow-up meeting at Trident."

"Thanks," Chet said. "Go get 'em."

 *Chapter Nine*

Chet looked up from the report he had been study-ing and smiled at both Carol and Duke.

"Duke, this is fantastic," he said, leaning back in his chair. "How did you do this?"

Duke beamed. "Pretty simple, actually. I met with Trident's production planning group yesterday and again today. Boy, were those eye-openers."

He got up and walked around as he spoke. "Turns out there's a new guy named Henry on their team, and he used our competitor at his old job. I'll bet you dollars to donuts that's where this whole thing got started."

Chet and Carol agreed.

"The thing is," Duke said, "Henry only used them for the easy offshore commodity work—long lead times on the cheap stuff." He paused to look at Chet. "And Henry also told me that our competi-tor had a product failure rate that was three times higher than ours, so there were always quality problems."

"Pretty much what we thought," Chet said.

"Anyway," Duke continued, "the big news is we looked at Trident's forecasts for the next twelve months, and there's a dramatic increase in the quan-tity and complexity of their precision components. So I picked up the phone and called Martina, our chief engineer, and twenty minutes later she was sitting with the Trident team, discussing how we could change the workflow to better meet their scheduling." Duke paused again before adding, "They think it could shave two days off their production schedule...and it won't cost us a dime. They all absolutely loved it, including Henry."

"That's some really nice work," Chet said, masking his excitement. He turned to Carol. "So how did your customer-service team do?"

Carol peered over her reading glasses. "Well, I learned a lot in the last couple days, too," she said. "I met with our contacts at Trident, and they really like how we're working with them. You were right about the new electronic billing system: they weren't happy with our delays, but now that it's working well, they're thrilled."

Chet nodded.

"I also asked them about how we could make it easier for them to place their orders," she continued. "They brought in someone from their IT department, and after talking it over, we found a way to streamline the work for both of us."

Carol's eyebrows drew together worriedly, sending her glasses farther down her nose. "The only problem is it will cost us fifty-thousand dollars to make the software changes."

Chet asked, "How much of a cost savings do you project for us if we make this change?"

"Hard to say," Carol answered with a shrug, "but I'd estimate we could get orders in the system twenty-four hours faster, eliminate manual-entry mistakes, and save on expedited freight costs."

Duke jumped in. "I like how we'd be fully integrated with their system, which would be a real competitive advantage. Plus, what's the cost of *not* doing it?"

"True, but fifty grand is a lot of Walt's money," Chet replied as he stood up and started pacing the room. "Let me digest that one. Carol, did you come up with anything else we should talk about in our presentation?"

"One more thing," she said. "I made a list of all the times our customer service team went above and beyond the call of duty." She handed Chet and Duke copies of the report. "As you can see, we jumped through a lot of hoops last year to make sure their orders were on track...especially when the delays were on their end."

Chet read through the list quickly and said, "Looks like we're building our case for why that B minus should be upgraded to an A. Carol, you and your team have done an incredible job, and same with you, Duke."

Chet walked around the room and absentmindedly stuck his hands in his pockets. When his fingers unexpectedly found a golf tee, a smile spread across his face. "Okay, let's take stock of our situation," he said. "We've re-prioritized and put all things Trident at the top of our lists. We've also examined how we can adapt from what we do now to what Trident really needs. As I see it, we have a lot of changes we need to make, and those include nearly every part of the company, so let's spend the rest of the day meeting with our people and getting them on board."

Wednesday, 6:15 P.M., AlphaMax Manufacturing

Chet sat at his desk and looked over his notes from the day. They'd made progress, no question, but worried thoughts still ran through his mind. *If I hear the words "that's not how we do it here" or "let me tell you why that won't work" or "that's not my job" again my head will explode. Carol and Duke get it, but we've only got one more day to get everyone in the company fully bought into the changes...I hope that's enough time.*

Having done all he could do at the moment, he shut down his computer, grabbed his keys, and headed for his final tune-up before the golf tournament.

 *Chapter Ten*

As Chet headed toward the clubhouse he saw Wayne, his brother-in-law, walking across the parking lot, already dressed in his golf shirt and shorts. Wayne had agreed to meet him for a quick nine holes as they prepped for Saturday's tournament. They chatted about the weather and then settled into some trash-talk.

"Duke and I are taking you and Reggie down," Wayne said.

Chet grinned. "I don't think so, my friend. As you will shortly see, I've fixed my putting problems, and that changes everything."

"Then hurry up and change clothes. I'll meet you at the first tee."

"I'll see you on the practice green in five minutes," Chet said. "The new Chet warms up."

Chet couldn't wait to put the old putter to the test on the links. There was a youthful exuberance in every step as he worked his way to his locker. This time when he opened the locker door he was actually looking forward to finding another card. He wasn't disappointed.

> be Responsible
> Take ownership of
> the outcome

This one caught him off guard. Be Responsible? He
flipped through the other cards to see if there was a
pattern:

> Prioritize
> Focus on what matters
> most

Adapt
See change as an opportunity

Each of the previous messages seemed to challenge him to reassess what he needed to do to improve his putting. That's exactly what he had been doing... wasn't it? He sat next to his locker for a moment thinking about the new message. *I am responsible for reading the green, for striking the ball, for sinking the putt. I can do it. It's up to me.*

Wednesday, 8:15 P.M., 9th Green, Meadowfield Golf Club

"That *can't* be right," said Wayne, grabbing the scorecard. While his brother-in-law re-did the math, Chet yanked the old putter from the bag, took off his golf glove, and tucked it in his back pocket.

Wayne tossed the scorecard onto the seat and got out of the cart. "It says here, *Chester*, that you only need to sink this putt to shoot a thirty-nine!" Wayne grabbed his putter and headed toward Chet on the green. "Excluding miniature golf, when was the last time you broke forty on nine holes?"

Chet laughed. "Quit trying to jinx me!"

The sun was low in the sky, casting long shadows that made it difficult to read the green. He took his time studying the putt.

Wayne pulled the flagstick and asked, "Want me to tend it?"

Chet shook his head. "No thanks, I think I've got it."

When he felt ready he took a practice stroke. *Ten feet, a little left to right break, slightly uphill.* He visualized the path the ball would take going in the hole.

By now, the old putter felt like a natural extension of his hands. With a confident motion he struck the ball. It rolled quickly toward the cup, slowed, curved right at the end, and plopped into the hole.

"Birdie!" Chet shouted, pumping his fist in the air. As he retrieved his ball he said, "Sorry about that bad golf etiquette. I probably should have let you tap in your eight-footer first."

Wayne gaped in disbelief. "If I hadn't seen it with my own two eyes…." After gathering himself he stood over his putt, stroked the ball, and drained it.

"Nice putt," Chet said as he offered a high-five. "Way to finish!"

"Thanks," Wayne said, "but unless you come back to earth on Saturday, it looks like the rest of us will be playing for second place."

 Chapter Eleven

Chet was on a roll. "If we didn't do it the way we do it now, how would you do it? If you could start from scratch, what would you do differently?" Chet looked straight at Oscar Brabonskowitz, AlphaMax's top information technology professional.

Oscar raised his eyebrows, clearly wondering what Chet expected.

"Trident is our number one customer," Chet said. "We need to approach this by thinking outside the box and focusing on *their* needs."

Oscar finally said, "I know you think we can just snap our fingers and do it, but programming takes time and money...and I'm not exactly swimming in either." Oscar clicked a few buttons on his computer and looked up at Chet. "Here's the deal: if we delayed the roll-out of the sales automation project, we could probably reassign some resources to Trident."

The sales automation effort had been Chet's pet project for the last two years, and it was finally ready to go live. "Do it," he said without hesitation. "I can't believe I'm telling you to back-burner the project I've been begging for, but that's what we need to do. Walt left me in charge, so *I'm* responsible for making sure we don't lose the Trident account, and we need to deliver some tangible value to them...*now.*"

Chet sat alone in his office, working on the Trident presentation. He felt both exhausted and exhilarated by the last few days. But mostly he felt proud of how the team had pulled together and accomplished so much so quickly.

As he wrote, something dawned on him. *The concepts that helped me improve my golf game are the same ones that we used to tackle the Trident crisis.* He smiled as he pondered the amazing parallels between the note cards in his locker and the business challenge at AlphaMax.

> <u>Prioritize.</u> Focus on what matters most.
> <u>Adapt.</u> See change as an opportunity.
> <u>Be Responsible.</u> Take ownership of the outcome.

It was like a light had just turned on and illuminated the entire situation. *By golly, I think tomorrow we're gonna do it!*

 ## Chapter Twelve

Chet was freaking out. He had never seen a presentation go so wrong. "What do you mean you're going to make some changes?" Reggie shouted. He was so mad he was spitting. "Why the heck didn't you do these things before?"

Reggie glared at the solemn faces surrounding the large mahogany table as he tried—unsuccessfully—to regain his composure. "If I had known all the things you weren't doing, I would have brought in your competitor a long time ago!"

Before Chet could respond, Duke jumped in. "What are you talking about?" he blurted out. "We've been busting our tails to help Trident, and all we get is you berating us for not acting faster! You have no idea how many times—"

"That's enough," Reggie shouted. He stood up from the table. "This meeting is over!" He turned to his Trident team. "Have our attorneys draw up the paperwork to invoke the early termination clause in the AlphaMax contract."

Chet leaped to his feet. "You can't do that! We'll do better! I promise we'll do better..."

"Wake up! Chet!" Grace, his wife, was shaking him. "Honey, you're having a nightmare."

Chet opened his eyes, surprised to find himself in his bedroom.

"Are you okay?" Grace asked.

He sat up in bed, rubbed his eyes, and looked at the clock: 3:10 A.M. "I dreamt we were in the Trident meeting and everything went terribly wrong," he said. "People were yelling and screaming and Reggie was firing us and—"

"You were only dreaming," his wife said. She rolled over and curled up with her pillow. "Go back to sleep. Don't worry, you'll do great tomorrow."

Chet lay down and tried to get comfortable, though his heart was still racing, his mind still spinning with the events of the dream. "I know I'll do great tomorrow," he said. "It's today I'm worried about."

Chapter Thirteen

Chet leaned back in his chair and took a deep breath. "I think we're ready." He looked at Carol and Duke. "How do you feel about the presentation?"

Carol spoke first. "I think it's terrific. We cover all the important points. It's strong and compelling. I'm not a golfer, but I even like the part about the putters. Let's hope they like it."

Duke nodded. "This is really good stuff. I like our odds."

Chet made a note as he listened. "I don't want to sound cocky, but my only concern now is what happens *after* we keep Trident. Has everyone at AlphaMax bought into the concept that we *all* own the solution, not just for Trident but for every one of our customers?"

Carol said, "We can't expect this to become part of our culture after a one-week crisis. The only way to engrain it is to repeat it. We need to reinforce how each of us is either selling to a customer, maintaining a customer, or delivering to a customer. And each of those functions is critical."

"And," Duke said, "that without a customer, nothing else really matters."

"Let's set a meeting for Monday morning to follow up so we don't lose the momentum we've established," Chet said. "And let's come up with the metrics we'll use to track our progress so we know where we stand on all of our key performance indicators. We need a clear list of what we're going to do, who's going to do it, and by when. Oh, and we also need to list what we're going to stop doing— to make sure we don't end up in a crisis like this again."

Carol and Duke agreed

"Let's meet at noon, grab a quick lunch, then head over to Trident," Chet said. "I'm driving."

 Chapter Fourteen

The boardroom was full. On one side of the large mahogany table sat six senior Trident executives, including Reggie Ward. On the other side: Chet, Carol, and Duke. Behind Chet, two golf clubs leaned against the meeting room wall.

Reggie opened the meeting with, "As you know, Trident is looking for ways to be more competitive, and we've asked one of our key suppliers, AlphaMax, to come here and present their ideas on how they can help us." Reggie looked at Chet. "So, with no further ado, I'll turn the floor over to Chet McGill."

Chet straightened his tie and walked to the end of the table. "Thank you for being here," he told the group in a confident tone. "The relationship between Trident and AlphaMax goes back many years, and we sincerely appreciate your business and the trust you have shown in us.

"Just a few days ago, we were content that everything was fine, that we were doing the best we possibly could for Trident. But the truth is we were plugged, stuck in our old way of doing things. So when we really dug into what mattered most to you — how we can help make you more competitive — we came up with some new ideas that we're going to share with you today.

"These ideas will change the way we do business, and change is never easy. But we have a team of winners who will do whatever it takes. People like Carol Hayes and her team of customer service partners, who in the last year worked forty-seven nights and weekends to make sure your orders arrived on time. People like Mike Duchovny and his production team, who worked diligently to exceed both the quality standards and delivery schedules that you established."

"Quality products. Superior service. Passionate people." Chet looked each Trident employee in the eye as he spoke. "These words are easy to say, but a lot harder to execute. So for the next few minutes we're going to show you our new ideas and reinforce our unique capabilities. In the end, we believe they all add up to AlphaMax being the right strategic partner for Trident.

"At this point, I'm going to turn the meeting over to Carol and Duke, who can go into greater detail on the ways we propose to improve efficiencies, boost your speed to market, and make you more competitive and better able to serve your customers."

Chet took his seat and listened intently as first Carol and then Duke articulated the plans to improve their already-good working relationship. The ideas were clear, the benefits real, and the response—judging from the questions and the body language on the other side of the table—was positive.

When it was time for Chet's closing comments, he again stood, but this time he spoke to his AlphaMax partners. "Thank you, Carol and Duke, well done. I really appreciate all of the hard work you and your teams put in to come up with these ideas."

Chet then turned to the other side of the table. "And to all of you at Trident, I also want to say thank you. Thank you for the business we have enjoyed, and thank you for challenging us to be our best."

Chet walked behind his seat and grasped the two golf clubs he had brought into the meeting. "You may have been wondering why I brought these putters to the meeting, so let me explain."

Holding up the Moonwalker 3000, he said, "I recently bought this fancy new one with the hope of getting an easy and instant improvement in my putting. Unfortunately, it didn't happen. As it turned out," he held up the old putter, "it's this old one that helped me lower my score. Sometimes new is better. But in this case, like most, the quick fixes aren't the answer. It always comes back to executing the fundamentals."

Chet stepped to the front of the boardroom. "We've done a lot of thinking and soul-searching recently, and I want to share three concepts that have helped shape how we approached this challenge."

"The first," Chet explained, "is prioritizing and focusing on what matters most. Here, our team worked closely with Trident to determine what we could do to enhance your competitiveness and prove that we are the lowest-total-cost vendor, not merely the cheapest. That was job number one, and it got our full attention."

"The second concept," he said, "is that we need to accelerate our ability to anticipate and adapt, because your needs are changing, and the rest of the world isn't standing still, either. As I said before, change is never easy, but because failure is such a lousy option, we're committed to making the changes we've outlined to produce more value for you."

Chet slung the old putter over his shoulder. "The third is to take responsibility and ownership of the outcome. For us, that means taking responsibility to do what's best for you, because in the long run, that's what's best for us. And it means we'll live up to our commitments, like following through on our promise to invest fifty-thousand dollars on the order integration system.

"In closing," Chet said earnestly, "I have two things I want to say. First, I apologize that it took a competitive situation for us to look so deeply at how we were doing things and at our relationship with you. That won't happen again. Second, I promise we'll rise to this challenge and do everything we can to help you improve your game." Chet paused and looked directly at Reggie. "I hope you have seen what you were looking for today and that we can continue to do great things together for many years to come. Thank you very much."

As the meeting broke up, Reggie approached Chet.

"Nice job," he said, extending his hand. "I think you surprised a few folks with both the passion in your message and all of your plans. You're really going to do all those things?"

"I will if you will."

"We're going to meet this afternoon to discuss

our options. We'll let you know our decision on Monday. Now, on to the next pressing matter at hand." Reggie picked up Chet's old putter. "What time do we tee off tomorrow?"

"Nine," Chet said. "I'll be there an hour early to warm up, so just look for the guy in the bright green alligator pants. And bring your 'A' game because I'm bringing that old putter, and I think we're gonna win."

 ## Chapter Fifteen

Chet arrived early at his locker and was bubbling with confidence. He was wearing his favorite shirt with the AlphaMax logo on it and was about to put on his golf shoes when he reached for the stack of note cards. He read through them for inspiration:

Prioritize
Focus on what matters most

Adapt
See change as an opportunity

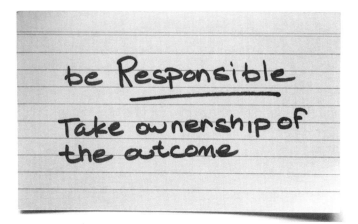

be Responsible
Take ownership of
the outcome

He locked on to the words "take ownership of
the outcome," and it gave him an extra shot of
enthusiasm. "That's right," Chet said as he slipped
his foot into the first shoe. "It's up to *me* to get this
done!"

"Talking to yourself again?" asked Doc Lanier,
who had come around the corner of the lockers.
"You ought to seek professional help," he groused
good-naturedly, adjusting his glasses. "And not just
for your game."

"Doc," Chet replied, lacing up his second shoe,
"*I* am responsible for playing my best so we can win
this darn tournament. So if you'll excuse me," he
said as he walked away, "I have some work to do."

The day's weather seemed to have been made
for golf: warm, a few light clouds, and just enough
breeze to spread the fragrance of honeysuckle across
the course. A gaggle of golfers were already check-

ing in, sipping coffee, and getting loose. As Chet walked toward the pro shop to get his bag, he saw Lou, the starter.

"Did you order up this great golfing weather?" Chet said. "If you did, you have my vote for the County Climate Control Board!"

Lou chuckled. "How's that Moonwalker 3000 working out for you?"

Chet adjusted his golf cap. "You know, it's the funniest thing. Remember that Par putter you told me to hang onto? Well, after struggling with the 3000, I thought I'd give that old one a try. And sure enough I've been putting lights out ever since. It's absolutely amazing."

Lou grinned knowingly. "That's great to hear! I knew you could do it if you just went back to the three basics." He took an abrupt look at his watch. "I need to do a couple of last-minute things before we get this show on the road, so just remember that par is a great score." He gave Chet a wink and added, "Good luck out there!"

Chet watched the spry older man hustle off, and turned to get his bag. Up ahead, under a banner that read "Meadowfield Golf Club Member-Guest Tournament," Chet saw a familiar face working the bag room.

"Howdy, Jack!" he said, reaching into his pocket and pulling out a crisp bill. "Here's ten bucks if you bring me my lucky golf bag."

Jack gave a mock military salute. "Lucky bag coming right up!"

Waiting for Jack to return, Chet looked around and saw Reggie putting his bag on their cart. The two exchanged waves just as Jack returned.

"You said your *lucky* bag, Mr. McGill?" said Jack.

"This is the one." Chet exchanged the bill for the bag and was about to head off before turning to Jack. "Do you know if anyone posted for that old putter?"

Jack shook his head. "I checked the board this morning and there's nothing about a missing putter."

Chet threw the bag strap over his shoulder and returned a mock salute to Jack. "All right then, carry on."

Saturday, 8:55 A.M., Meadowfield Golf Club

"Attention golfers!" boomed the voice of head pro Burt Gregory over portable speakers. "We are ready to get started. Please assemble at the first tee."

Chet glanced at Reggie and asked, "Are you warmed up?"

Reggie putted his last ball and watched it roll ten feet into the heart of the cup. He looked up with a smile. "Yeah, I'm ready."

"Don't leave it on the practice green," Chet said, stashing the ball in his pocket. "Let's head over."

A large crowd had already gathered at the first tee. Burt Gregory cleared his throat and spoke into the microphone.

"Welcome again, everyone, to the Meadowfield Golf Club Member-Guest Tournament. We have a terrific day planned for you, including beautiful weather and some really big trophies."

The crowd applauded.

"Before we get started, let me go over a few rules. It's a shotgun start, and the hole you begin on is listed on your cart. As far as scoring goes, we have two games. One is low gross and the other is low net. A low-gross trophy goes to the person and also team with the lowest actual scores. The low-net trophies go to the player and team with the lowest scores after we subtract your handicap. So if you shoot a ninety, and your handicap is eighteen, that's a net seventy-two."

Burt paused a moment. "And for you guests who shoot a seventy-five and report a handicap of eighteen, I'm going to have a long conversation with your home course head pro." He used the same line every year, and it always drew a laugh. "Good luck, have fun, and head out to your tees."

Chet glanced at the sign on their cart, then at Reggie. "Looks like we start here on number one," he said, assuming his game face.

Reggie grinned, adding, "I'm taking that as a good omen."

Chet smiled. "Yeah, that's a good sign." He checked his right pocket: ball marker, tee, and ball repair. *Check.* "Oh, and I have something for you."

Chet handed Reggie a sleeve of golf balls. "These are from my private stash, virtually guaranteed to stay in bounds."

Reggie took out a ball and examined it. "Very nice. It must have taken you hours to paint the AlphaMax logo on each one. And speaking of AlphaMax, it goes without saying that while I appreciate you inviting me to play in this tournament, business is business and golf is golf. This won't have any bearing on our decision."

"Of course not," Chet said. "And given my erratic game, I'm actually glad to hear that."

"Hey, Duke! Look who we're paired up with!" Wayne Davidson bellowed as he rolled his cart next to Chet's. "Christmas, Thanksgiving, birthday parties…I just can't get rid of this guy."

"I think you married my wife's little sister just so you could spend more time with me," Chet said.

The foursome exchanged friendly banter before getting ready to start.

Chet took Reggie aside and said, "Tell me what you think of this plan: let's really work hard to stay within our games. If we take a bad swing, let's not go for a miracle shot to recover. Just play for a bogey. Bogies won't kill us, but triple bogies will."

"It's like you said yesterday: focus on what matters most," Reggie replied with steely determination. "And today that's winning."

Chet nodded and took a deep breath. *I'm not*

going to let the pressure get to me. It's only a tourna-
ment. And I'm only playing with the decision-maker
who controls the 20 percent of our business that we
will either retain or lose on Monday. And he really
wants to win.

Chet began nervously counting his clubs.
Fourteen—including his two putters—the maximum
allowed. As his anxiety subsided he paused a moment, pulled out the Par putter, and reflected on
how far he had come in the past few days.

"A week ago I thought my new Moonwalker
3000 was going to turn my putting game around," he
told Reggie. "But it wasn't until I found this old putter and went back to the basics that I started making
some progress." He shook his head. "I'm starting to
think this thing is magic. How crazy is that?"

Reggie grinned and said, "As long as you're
draining 'em, I don't care if you go Happy Gilmore
and use a hockey stick."

Just then a distant horn signaled the start of play.

Reggie, looking very determined, said, "That's
our cue."

"Let's win this thing," Chet responded.

 Chapter Sixteen

"I think you're away, Reggie," Duke said as his opponent lined up his putt. "Make sure you dial a 'one' before you hit it, because that's definitely long distance."

Reggie eyed his shot as Chet tended the pin. "Looks like it's going to break left at the end," Chet advised.

Reggie nodded, settled in over his ball, and gave it a spank. It rolled swiftly across the width of the green, bent left, and ended up two feet short of the hole. "Outstanding!" Chet said as he laid down the flagstick out of the way. "Tap that in for a par."

"You guys are *killing* me," Duke intoned as he crouched to examine the twenty feet between his ball and the cup. "I blast my drive thirty yards past you guys, and now I need to sink this just to salvage a bogie."

"Quit griping and drain it," Wayne said testily. "We need it."

Duke readied himself and sent the ball toward the cup. It rolled up a slight ridge and plopped squarely in the hole. "*Yes!* It's about time one of those dropped in," he said with a grin. "Come on, Wayne. We need yours, too."

Wayne nodded and gave his sixteen-footer a final examination. After a practice stroke, he addressed the ball and gave it a rap. The ball sped directly toward the target, slammed into the back of the hole, popped up in the air, and came to rest two inches from the cup. "Ahhhh, darn it!" he yelled.

"You know I'd normally give you that putt," Chet said.

Wayne shot Chet a glance as he walked over and tapped in his ball. "There. Now let's see if you can handle the pressure. You *are* putting for a front-nine score of forty, aren't you?"

"As a matter of fact, I am," Chet said, calmly studying his shot. Reggie crouched a few feet behind him.

"Looks straight as an arrow to me," Reggie said quietly.

Chet nodded almost imperceptibly and took a practice stroke. He ran through his pre-putt mantra: analyze the distance, break, and slope, then visualize the ball going in. Settling into a comfortable grip, he stood over the ball and stroked the putt. The ball rolled straight toward the hole and dropped in the right side of the cup.

Chet smiled and gave the putter a kiss. "I love this club."

"I'm starting to get a little fond of it myself," added Reggie as he high-fived Chet. "We're halfway home. Let's keep it going."

"I've got you down for a forty-one, so with my score, I think the good guys are in the lead."

Nine more holes, Chet thought. *Hang in there.*

 **Chapter Seventeen**

As they approached the pro shop, Chet stopped the cart and got out. "As long as we're here at the turn, I'm going to go inside and powder my nose," he told Reggie. "Will you grab me an iced tea at the snack shack?"

"Sure thing," Reggie said. "You take the cart. I'll grab my driver and meet you at the tenth tee."

A couple minutes later, as Chet walked down the hall from the men's room and past the counter at the pro shop, he overheard the words "lost putter." He stopped in his tracks, and, with a sudden dread, turned his attention to a man talking with a club worker.

"My uncle is flying home tonight, and he'd really like to take his putter with him," the man said. "It doesn't look like much, just an old-fashioned putter with a wooden shaft and a leather grip. He lost it somewhere on the course last week."

Chet listened in stunned silence as the pro shop employee said she would look for it in the lost-and-found bin.

That's the putter in my bag, Chet thought. *My putter. The reason I'm playing the best golf of my life!*

He paced an aisle of the pro shop, running options through his head. *I could keep the putter until after the tournament and then turn it in. No one knows I overheard the conversation, and the uncle probably could live without it for a couple days. Besides, maybe "my" putter isn't the same one he's looking for.* Chet fidgeted as he thought. *Or I could turn it in now.*

The last idea sent chills up his spine. *Switch back to the Moonwalker 3000, right now, in the middle of the tournament? The putter I couldn't putt with? At a time when it mattered most? Possibly dashing all hope of winning the tournament and jeopardizing my most important customer relationship?*

Chet drew a deep breath. He had to decide *now.*

Saturday, 11:50 A.M., 10th Tee, Meadowfield Golf Club

Chet raced the cart up to the tenth tee, came to an abrupt stop, and hopped out.

"What took you so long?" Wayne chided. "Trying on new clothes at the pro shop?"

Chet snatched his driver from his bag and hustled to the tee box. "I had a little problem."

"I told you to quit eating those breakfast burritos," Duke said, prompting a laugh from Wayne.

"Not that kind of a problem," Chet replied somberly. "I overheard someone in the pro shop saying his uncle lost an old wood-shafted putter."

"Ooo...bad timing," Wayne said with mock concern. "You were really starting to like that putter. You even kissed it. So are you going to turn it in?"

Chet was ready to hit his drive. He took his

quirky backswing and lashed at the ball, sending it far down the right side. It sliced a little, took a bad bounce, and ended up under a tree.

"I already did," Chet finally replied.

Wayne was flabbergasted. "You turned in your magic putter?" Wayne put his arm around Duke and said, "Partner, I think we just got a second chance. The old Chet is back!" The two drove off, laughing.

Chet got in the cart and started to drive.

"Where's your ball?"

"In the fairway, up near your ball." Reggie sat silently, then added, "That must have been a tough decision."

Chet nodded. "Harder than it should have been. I'd been playing so well with that old putter." Chet glanced at Reggie with a concerned look in his eyes. "I really wanted to give us our best chance of winning this tournament, so I apologize in advance if this is the reason we end up losing."

"Stop the cart," Reggie demanded. "Stop the cart!"

Chet braked hard. Reggie put his hand on Chet's shoulder and spoke commandingly. "We are still going to win this, you hear? Turning in the putter was the right thing to do, and your game is not going to fall apart because of it. That was *you* knocking in those clutch putts on the front nine, not the putter. It's like you said yesterday: now's the time to stay focused on your priorities, adapt to the new putter, and take responsibly for your game. You with me?"

Chet smiled. "I'm with you." He accelerated the

cart to its top speed and drove a few moments before speaking again, this time with renewed vigor. "Sometimes you have to focus on what you want instead of what you want to avoid. And I want our names engraved on that trophy."

 ## Chapter Eighteen

Chet reached into his bag, pulled out the Moonwalker 3000, and walked toward the green. It seemed like forever since he'd last used it.

Reggie was right, Chet thought. *I was the one sinking the putts, not the putter. And I was the one who had prioritized, adapted, and taken responsibility for the outcome. I can do this.*

Duke looked up from fixing his ball mark on the green. "What are you putting for?"

"I've got a twenty-footer for par," Chet replied. "It's time to see how my new putter does the second time around."

"Just get close enough to give me a good read, will you?" cracked Duke.

Chet was away, the farthest from the pin, and so he hit first. He carefully read the green: he had an uphill putt that looked to break two feet to the left. The greens had dried out and were lightning fast.

"Punch it in," Reggie urged.

As Chet took a couple practice strokes he noted that the Moonwalker 3000 looked totally different from the old putter but had a similar well-balanced feel. *Time to adapt my smooth stroke to my new putter.* He recalled the old putter's three lines and their message: assess the distance, break, and slope. He carefully settled in over the ball and gave it a whack.

The ball danced up the slope, curved left, and came to rest three inches from the hole.

"Way to go!" Reggie exclaimed. "You da man!"

Chet beamed. "I'm happy to say that the reports of my demise have been greatly exaggerated."

Saturday, 2:45 P.M., 18th Fairway, Meadowfield Golf Club

"Okay, partner," Reggie said, "let's take stock of our situation. I'm one-hundred-and-fifty yards out with a good lie in the fairway. If I can knock it on the green and two-putt, I'll finish with an eighty-two. With my handicap, that would be a net sixty-six."

Chet nodded. "Pretty darn good. You can do it." Chet pulled out an eight iron. "I've got one-hundred-and-thirty-eight yards to go. With a two-putt, I'd card an eighty-three. Subtract my handicap and that's a net sixty-five. The bottom line is if we both get a par we have a great chance of winning, so let's finish strong."

"You got that right," Reggie said, addressing his ball. He put a good swing on his seven iron and sent the ball soaring toward the green. It landed on the front fringe and bounced onto the short grass.

"Beautiful shot," Chet said, walking to his ball. "Let's see if I can get inside that."

He took a practice swing, settled the blade behind the ball, and gave it a rip. "Darn it all," Chet exclaimed, "I yanked it!" The ball flew toward the left of the green and settled in the rough between two sand traps.

"At least you're not in a bunker," Reggie said. "The way you're playing you can get up and down from there."

Chet slid his club back in the bag with a little extra oomph. "This game's never easy, is it?"

They hopped back in the cart and drove to the green. Wayne and Duke were already on the green surveying their shots. "So who's the lucky dog with the tough lie over there in the rough?" asked Duke.

"That would be this bulldog here," Chet said as he went looking for his ball. He found it buried deep in the long grass, three paces off the green and fifty long, downhill feet from the flag.

After mulling over his club selection he chose his sand wedge. The idea was to take a firm swing to get through the deep rough. *Just get it on the green*, Chet thought.

He steadied himself and swung. The ball popped up in the air, landed on the fringe, and rolled down the slope. It came to rest twelve feet from the hole, leaving a tricky downhill putt to finish.

"Good shot, but there's still a lot of meat on that bone," jabbed Wayne.

Chet set his wedges off to the side of the green, marked his ball, and watched as Duke's long putt ended up two feet from the cup.

"Great putt," Chet said. "Way to finish. What's that give you?"

Duke said, "I'll tap that in for a ninety-one, net seventy-one." He shrugged. "I'll take it."

It was Reggie's turn. He was staring at a tricky thirty-footer that broke sharply left. "Come on, Reggie," Chet said. "You can drain it."

Reggie gave the ball a poke and watched as it rolled a foot past the cup.

"That's my, partner!" Chet exclaimed. "Great par."

Reggie tapped the ball in, retrieved it without stepping on Wayne's line, and walked over to Chet. The pair watched as Wayne pushed his fifteen-foot putt to the right and tapped it in for a bogey.

"Thank goodness this round is over," Wayne said. "Ninety-seven, net seventy-five. That and five bucks gets me a beer."

Chet was finally up. He placed his ball in front of his marker and stepped back to give it a final analysis. "Looks severely downhill with a six-inch break to the right at the end," he said, turning to Reggie.

Reggie stood up from his crouch and nodded. "It's going to pick up a lot of speed, so just get it started a little left and let it hit the cup."

Chet approached the ball and took a feather-like practice stroke. As he considered his shot one last time he thought back to the words on one of the note cards: "take ownership of the outcome." In his mind's eye, he watched the ball roll in the hole. *I am responsible for sinking this putt.*

He finally settled in over his ball. As if in slow motion, Chet drew back his Moonwalker 3000 and gave the ball a nudge. It quickly picked up speed, caught the break, and slammed into the cup.

"Yes!" Reggie shouted as he gave Chet a hug. "That was unbelievable! What a round!"

"You guys tore it up today," Wayne said, shaking hands with Chet and Reggie.

"Thanks," Chet replied. "You and Duke held your own, too."

As they walked off the green, Chet threw his arm around Reggie's shoulder. "You played awesome out there. And thanks for that pep talk on ten. It made the difference."

Reggie turned to Chet. "No, thank *you*. You showed me a lot today. I saw your grit and determination in the clutch. But mostly I saw that when the pressure was on, you did the right thing and turned in the old club...then overcame the challenge with your new putter."

Chet was almost embarrassed at the compliment. "I really appreciate that." He paused and added with a smile, "That's the way we AlphaMax folks roll."

Reggie looked at Chet. "As a matter of fact, that *is* how your AlphaMax team rolls. You really practice what you preach: you prioritize and focus on what matters most, you adapt and change, and you take responsibility for the outcome...even if it means losing a golf tournament."

"It's not just talk," Chet said. "We walk the walk."

"You know," Reggie said, "I have a feeling Monday might be another good day for you. As a matter of fact, Monday might be good for everyone at AlphaMax...but don't tell anyone I told you that."

Chet smiled broadly. "I can't tell you how good that is to hear! But don't worry, your intuition's safe with me."

Reggie gave Chet a friendly slap on the shoulder. "C'mon. Let's pack up and check the leader board."

As they walked toward the gathering crowd near the clubhouse, Chet heard his name called. He turned and saw Jack approaching him. "Glad I found you, Mr. McGill," he said handing Chet a piece of paper. "Lou asked me to give you this."

Chet's quizzical expression quickly turned to a broad smile as he read the note:

It wasn't the putter—
you just went back to
the basics.
Well done!
Lou

"Fan mail," Chet said to Reggie as he put his tees, balls, and the note card in his golf bag. Then he felt his cell phone vibrating in one of the pockets. He fished it out and looked at the number: it was Walter Murdock, AlphaMax's president.

Chet pressed the talk button. "Hey, Walt, welcome back! How was your vacation?"

"Absolutely incredible," Walt said. "I can't believe how quickly I got used to not hearing the phone ring. I'll tell you all about it when I'm back in the office. So how did things go last week?"

"Just business as usual," Chet said, shooting a smile at Reggie. "In fact, I'd call it PAR for the course."

 *The 19th Hole*

Chet received three insights during the course of the story:

> **Prioritize.** Focus on what matters most.
> **Adapt.** See change as an opportunity.
> **Be Responsible.** Take ownership of the outcome.

These guiding principles form an easy-to-remember acronym: PAR.

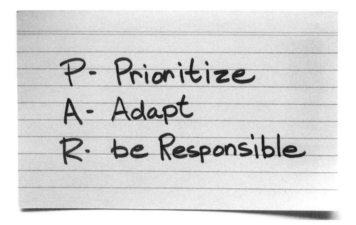

By keeping these PAR thoughts in mind and sharing them with your team, you will dramatically improve your odds of succeeding in business, life, and golf. Plus, these concepts will help you overcome challenges and get the right things done.

The word "par" has several meanings.

In financial circles, it's the issued value of a bond or a share of stock.

In a dictionary, it's the average level or normal standard.

In golf, it's the standard of excellence!

The truth is, few people shoot par over a round of golf. In fact, only a handful of the world's best golfers average below par any given year. Just like par in golf is a lofty goal, PAR should be your organization's standard for baseline performance.

A word of caution: don't get paralyzed by the pursuit of perfection. It's better to have a *good* strategy that gets fully implemented quickly than a *perfect* strategy that never gets off the ground. Your goal should be to get the *right* things done because that's how you *win*.

The order in which you do these PAR steps is important. You likely have dozens of issues and challenges, but you can't take them on all at once. Narrow your list to the ones that absolutely, positively have to get done. Once you have your priorities, you'll know what needs to change. As you and your team go through this process, you'll develop buy-in and the resulting responsibility for the outcome.

General George S. Patton said, "A good plan executed now is better than a great one executed next week." The key is to take action and keep it simple. Let's take a closer look at each PAR idea in the context of business, golf, and your personal life.

> **Prioritize**. Focus on what matters most.

Business: It almost goes without saying that getting the most important things done is critical to the success of any organization, but the truth is that it's a lot harder to keep that focus amid all the distractions. And in today's difficult economic climate, that truth has never been truer. In tough times, the weak fail, and the strong position themselves for future growth. The difference between the two often comes down to whether leadership had the ability to focus the entire organization's attention on the things that are really most important.

Long-term success is the ultimate goal for every business, so job number one for every leader is making sure they're headed in the right direction. The heart of that process is identifying the specific initiatives and issues that need the most focus. For a service company, the number one priority may be reducing turnover to improve customer service levels. For a manufacturing company, it may be to develop a new technology to leapfrog competitors with improved quality or lower costs. For a distributor, it may be to open new distribution centers or find new market niches. In every case it comes down to being focused on what your *customers* are saying.

In difficult times, many companies are forced to

shift from a long-term focus to merely surviving the short term. This "live to fight another day" approach means making painful decisions to ensure the organization survives. During times like these, there is no more important job than having a sharp focus on what matters most.

But prioritizing is not just for the mega-issues. Prioritization cascades from strategic objectives to action steps. A sales manager may need to focus on boosting the number of face-to-face presentations to increase sales. An accounts receivable manager may need to streamline workflow to increase the number of collection calls. And a warehouse manager may need to reorganize the layout of the racking to improve the output of a pick-and-pack process.

Let's take a look at some examples of how major companies have used prioritizing to create a competitive advantage. Procter & Gamble is well known as the world's largest consumer-products company and the owner of such successful brands as Tide detergent, Pampers diapers, and Ivory soap. P&G's strategy is clear: focus on products that can create a new category or on products that can be category leaders because they represent measurable advantages to the consumer. Plus they focus on categories with high-growth potential, as those will help the company expand faster than its competitors.

With this well-defined focus, P&G sold brands like Jif peanut butter, Comet cleanser, Prell shampoo, and Sunny Delight beverages. Meanwhile, the company poured millions into research and development of high-potential products like Febreze, Pantene, and Olay. They made major acquisitions, such as Iams, Gilette, and Oral B. The result? Dramatic growth in sales and profits.

Another company that has benefited from a sharp focus is ING Direct. With no fees, no minimums, and attractive interest rates, they have become one of the fastest-growing providers of checking accounts in America. But what's unusual about ING Direct is their focus: they will not accept large deposits because they refuse to treat big customers differently than regular customers, and they refuse to offer credit cards because they believe people have too much debt.

ING's approach is to keep it simple and focus on ways to do things quickly and with low overhead. They have refused to add brick-and-mortar branches, ATMs, financial advisors, or commercial bankers. Critics used to say they were leaving millions of dollars on the table, but after the recent banking crisis, ING's sharp focus is now a blueprint for not only survival but for long-term success.

Business leaders need to make these types of strategic decisions their highest priority and not allow daily distractions to shift their focus. How? Set time aside when you only address the most important decisions. This can be an annual retreat, off-site quarterly meetings, weekly reviews, or whatever seems appropriate for your situation, including some quiet concentrated time each day.

Consider the following questions to help identify your highest priorities:

- What are the top three goals we want to accomplish?

- What are the most significant trends that will impact our markets over the next five years?

- What are our most pressing short-term and long-term threats?

- Are we properly positioned to attract, retain, and motivate our number one competitive advantage, our employees?

- What emerging markets offer significant growth opportunities and leverage our current strengths?

- What are we doing to develop technological competitive advantages?

- Is our corporate vision statement engrained in our culture, and does it send us in the right direction?

As you develop your priorities, keep these thoughts in mind:

- A vision statement guides your overall direction. It's what you want to be.

- A mission statement guides your overall purpose. It's why you exist.

- Strategic plans specifically lay out what you want to accomplish and how you want to use your resources. It's your game plan of what success looks like.

- Tactical plans specifically say how you will accomplish your plans on a day-to-day basis.

- Goal statements are the milestones by which you measure your results.

- Your dashboard is how you track your key metrics to ensure you stay focused on your priorities.

Prioritizing is also important on a smaller scale. The hourly question of *what should I do next?* should always be answered by thinking first *what is my highest priority?* A great way to do this is to break down your top two to three strategic initiatives into detailed action steps with due dates and metrics. If you do these activities and hit your progress dates, the results will follow. Keep this front and center in some form whether it's an Excel or Word template, calendar with Post-It notes, or project management software program. Assign a number to indicate priority and then get going on your number ones.

Allow time for interruptions and the occasional crisis. Weave a few "quick and easys" into the mix so that when you work on a piece of a number one you can focus solely on it for enough time to make real progress, or even get it done.

Beware of the time zappers: emails, incoming phone calls, meetings, and other things can take your eye off the ball. One strategy to manage your time is to set aside certain blocks of the day to do administrative tasks and other times to focus just on your top initiatives' activities. Maybe you only check email three times a day: at the start, at lunch, and before you leave. The bottom line: don't be incredibly busy doing nonproductive things.

Another way to look at prioritizing is to make sure your time, talent, and resources are spent on your top initiatives. Think of time as money. If you spend it on an activity, what aren't you able to do (or buy) in exchange? In the end, it's all about focusing on what matters most.

Golf: If you slice the heck out of every tee shot, but the rest of your game is okay, it might be a good idea to show up for your lessons with your driver in hand. Let's face it: the game isn't much fun when you spend more time looking for your ball than hitting it. Legendary golfer Ben Hogan said, "Your first shot on every hole is the most important, because all the others essentially depend on the quality of the first."

Golf is an exceedingly complex game, with many interrelated elements. For example, if you have difficulty getting off the tee with your driver, that might be a symptom of a flaw in your swing, grip, or stance. In most cases a few lessons from a pro will help you identify the problem. Then it's up to you to focus on that specific aspect and practice until the solution becomes second nature.

In Chet's case, his challenge was putting. He kept looking for quick fixes, but there aren't many of those on the links. He only saw significant improvement after he put a priority on his putting, concentrated on a proven methodology, and practiced.

Life: Here, you set your own priorities about your dreams and what you want to accomplish. The idea is to think about what in your personal life is most important and needs focus. It may be your marriage, children, finances, something spiritual, volunteer work, personal growth, a physical goal, or your health. Whatever it is, make your decision and give it the attention it deserves. This can be difficult because all of these areas are number ones for most of us, and each area needs attention regularly. Though they don't all need the same quantity of time, neglecting any will eventually result in long-term losses.

You'll do your best work when the rest of your life is in balance, so put your top personal priorities on a list, commit yourself to accomplishing them, and develop an action plan on how you're going to do them. You can't change the past, but you can change the future...if you know what you want.

> **Adapt.** See change as an opportunity.

Business: The business world is changing so fast it's mind-boggling. One generation ago, college graduates entered into a business world that had no personal computers, no Internet, no cell phones, no fax machines, no DVDs, and—most startling—no Starbucks. How anyone did business is still a mystery, but the point is that everything is continuing to change at a blistering pace. There's unrelenting pressure to do things faster, better, cheaper.

To compete and win in business, companies need to make sure they keep looking a few years down the road. Find new ways to serve customers. Reorganize your company to eliminate wasted effort. Merge with a competitor. Move into new markets.

The best firms foster an environment that encourages innovation, regardless of how small the change. Once this spirit of innovation is engrained in your culture, you will move faster, build loyalty among your employees, and discover new ways to stay ahead of the competition.

There are numerous examples of companies that have won not only by adapting to a changing environment but also changing the environment itself. Apple Computer applied their uncanny ability to simplify electronics to the personal music field and created the iPod, a product that revolutionized the music industry and dramatically grew the company. That innovation, in turn, led them to create the iPhone, a product that is changing the way people communicate.

How did Apple turn a niche computer maker into the hottest tech company on the planet? They started at the top by rehiring founder Steve Jobs. As one of the great innovators of his generation, Jobs was always looking for new ways to invent (iTunes music downloads) or reinvent (Pixar digital films, now part of Disney) everything he touched. Who at your company is challenging and championing your efforts to leverage your strengths and reinvent your business?

Toyota is the world's largest car company and in 2008 overtook General Motors for the number-one position in the U.S. auto market. One of the reasons for their success is their ability to adapt to changes in the marketplace. For example, consider their Lexus brand. Introduced in 1989, it has become the best-selling luxury car line in the U.S., besting the well-established Cadillac, Lincoln, Mercedes, and BMW brands.

In the 1990s, Toyota saw a growing trend toward better fuel economy and an increased concern for the environment. Their drive to adapt to a changing world led them to introduce the Prius hybrid car in 2000, well before other auto manufacturers. The world's first mass-produced hybrid is now one of the hottest-selling cars in North America, in part due to their early leadership in "green" technology. And Toyota has successfully taken that same technology and applied it to their popular Camry and Highlander vehicles.

Spotting trends and adapting to them has long been a strong suit for McDonald's, the world's largest fast-food company. Where would they be without the Egg McMuffin (which virtually invented the fast-food breakfast market), their successful line of salads (which put McDonald's in synch with health-conscious Americans), and their line of premium coffees?

Another example of McDonald's ability to adapt is the story of the Filet-O-Fish. In 1962, Lou Groen, the owner of the first McDonald's franchise in Cincinnati, was struggling with hamburger sales during Lent in his largely Catholic market. He dealt with the situation by creating the Filet-O-Fish sandwich, a product he credited for saving his business. Meanwhile back in Chicago, McDonald's founder, Ray Kroc, had his own idea for a sandwich to sell to nonmeat eaters: the Hula Burger, a pineapple slice on a bun. Kroc decided to test the two new products head to head, and the one that sold the most would roll out nationwide. You probably know how the test ended up, since McDonald's now sells three-hundred-million Filet-O-Fish sandwiches a year. Is your company cooking up a winning recipe when faced with a challenge?

Or take Pepsi. After watching the explosive growth of bottled water, they could have fought the trend with their flagship cola or Mountain Dew. Instead, they created Aquafina and rode the wave, along the way creating the best-selling brand of bottled water in America.

It is easy to see the mistakes of the old-time businesses that didn't adapt: the buggy and wagon makers who didn't move into cars, the railroads who didn't get into the airline industry, the phonograph companies who didn't go into radio. But what about today? What are the businesses that ten or twenty years from now people will be saying, "Why didn't someone see this opportunity sooner?"

The companies that adapt fastest to changes in the marketplace are often the ones that win in the long run. An ingrained spirit of innovation and constant improvement are the twin cornerstones of your future. Business leaders need to paint the picture for employees to help overcome the natural resistance to change. How? Talk with them, share your vision, and most importantly, let them know that change means taking chances.

Listening skills are particularly critical as you build a culture of change. This is most important when dealing with people who are not your age or come from a different background, as their view of the world may be quite different from yours. See what you can learn from their perspective and how that can apply to the challenge you face.

The coffee industry provides a great example of this approach. In 1987, the big three brands (Procter & Gamble's Folgers, General Foods' Maxwell House, and Nestle's Nescafé) held 90 percent of the market share. Coffee was an adult drink, mostly consumed at home or in restaurants. But consumer preferences began to change. Gourmet brands and coffee houses flourished as coffee went from stodgy to hip. Starbucks, once a local Seattle coffee roaster, quickly became the eight-hundred-pound gorilla. Could the coffee powerhouses from the 1980s have altered their fates if they had adapted quicker—and listened more closely—to a changing marketplace?

Make sure you aren't a frog. These amphibians, as you may recall from high school biology class, are cold-blooded animals. If you put a frog in a small pan with one inch of water—and we are not suggesting you actually do this...just take our word for it—and put the pan over a burner on the stove, the frog won't sense the gradual change in temperature. Even though the frog could easily jump out of the pan at any time, if it doesn't eventually sense it's in hot water, it will be too late.

Make sure you develop your ability to sense change early so you have time to adapt to it, because you can't adapt to a changing environment if you don't know it exists. Keep your antenna up. Critical to the process is to let your partners know that the best thing for everyone in the long run is to get ahead of the change curve and see change as an opportunity.

Golf: Tiger Woods decided to totally rebuild his swing—twice—after he had won the Masters and a fistful of professional tournaments. Why? He didn't think his swing was good enough to take him where he wanted to go and recognized the need to keep improving.

Adapting to new circumstances is an integral part of the game of golf. Whether it's high winds, a new course with lots of water, or even an aching hamstring, successful golfers know they need to be able to change to win.

Chet knew he had to make some changes in his putting or he wouldn't be able to lower his scores. He tried a new putter, but that didn't give him the instant fix he wanted. He then changed the way he approached his putting. He really thought about the conditions he faced and made sure he considered everything he had learned before stroking his putt.

This worked because it was fundamentally sound and he resolved to make it work. You can do the same.

Life: You and the world around you are changing. Successful people learn fast and use change to their advantage.

You must embrace new technology, ideas, and changing times. And look at changing yourself. What should you improve? What would have the most impact on your life, and where can you grow?

If this openness to change doesn't come naturally, you're going to have to push yourself. Get up thirty minutes earlier to work out, try Thai food, work in the garden, check out that new gadget, or listen to modern music even though these ideas don't appeal to you. Listen to what others say about you. Does their perception match your picture of yourself?

If you approach new things with an open mind and a good attitude, you'll be surprised at how many things you enjoy (or at least accept) that were once outside your comfort zone.

> **Be Responsible.** Take ownership of the outcome.

Business: Here's a little tip: in the short sprint for power and money, you really don't have to smile, hold the door open for grandmothers, or even have a shred of decency. But a business career isn't a short sprint; it's a marathon. Customers actually do remember the people who do whatever it takes to give great service. And they stay with them.

Responsibility starts at the top of your company and flows down to the frontline workers. Companies that take responsibility for caring about their customers, their employees, and their communities *will* do better in the long run.

Businesses need to earn a profit, but the days are gone when they can ignore their impact on the environment, the safety of their products, and the well-being of their employees. In today's world these are non-negotiable issues, and any organization that refuses to accept them will have to deal with the painful consequences. And as Chet discovered when he returned the putter, making the tough call often turns out well in the end.

Headlines of wrongdoing are more sensational (and probably sell more magazine copies), but there are many examples of companies that have quietly taken responsibility for doing the right thing...and benefited from it.

Google is the most popular search engine in the world and is ranked one of the best companies to work for in America. It's not just because their stock has historically performed well (although that certainly has helped), but also in part because of how well they treat their employees.

Google says, "Give the proper tools to a group of people that want to make a difference, and they will." The company's goal is to "strip away anything that gets in the employee's way," and they do that with first-class dining facilities, gyms, car washes, laundry facilities...even massage areas. Has your company taken responsibility for rubbing your employees the *right* way?

Nike is now not only the top athletic shoe company in the world, but a leading sporting goods and apparel company as well. They took a multi-million-dollar inventory loss when they severed ties with football star Michael Vick over his dog-fighting scandal. One could argue that they were forced to drop Vick and their decision was merely a shrewd business decision. But the reality is that taking responsibility to do the right thing sometimes means taking a painful step back to ensure the long-term viability of the brand.

Another example of taking responsibility is Cintas, one of America's most respected business services companies (and in the spirit of full disclosure, the employer of one of this book's co-authors). As the nation's largest renter of business uniforms, Cintas uses a lot of soap to wash shirts and pants for its five million customers. Despite higher costs, the company recently switched to a new environmentally friendly detergent formula. Is your company ready to clean up by doing the right thing?

We've all read how Enron, Arthur Andersen, WorldCom, and others crashed and burned because they simply didn't take responsibility to do what's right. Make sure your organization is never included in this list. How? By letting everyone know what you stand for and reinforcing those values every chance you get. If you simply do what you say you're going to do, people will trust you and your organization... and that approach will reflect in your culture and bottom line.

Responsibility in business is also a personal thing. Every employee has to take ownership for their individual work. This means making sure the project that is due on Friday gets done by Friday... no matter what it takes. Only when every player on your team takes their individual responsibility personally will the entire organization thrive.

True responsibility also means not just *talking* about what you're going to do but *taking action* on it and *being accountable for the results.* The bottom line is that people understand what it means to "own the outcome." It doesn't matter whether it's a person or a company that owns a result—the same principles apply.

Individual owners need to understand that they are the *only* ones responsible for the outcome, even if they are working with others to produce the results. In our story, Chet was responsible for AlphaMax keeping the Trident business even though he relied on Carol, Duke, and the entire team. Merrill Lynch's former CEO Stan O'Neal lost his job because the company wrote off $4.5 billion in bad debt, and O'Neal ultimately shouldered the blame even though he didn't personally make those bad investments.

A key factor in responsibility is following through and following up. *Following through* means doing what you say you're going to do when you say you're going to do it. *Following up* is holding others accountable by checking in on their progress and helping them when they're stuck. Remember, the goal is to achieve success for the company or the initiative. You only achieve success if everyone does their part. It's not good enough for just you to have crossed the finish line.

Definitive action plans and progress metrics need to be established to ensure progress is on track. It is here that the "owners" hold themselves and each other accountable for results. There are several good templates to use as resources, including the time-tested OGSM (Objectives, Goals, Strategies & Measures) model used by Procter & Gamble, Toyota, and many other successful organizations. Additional resources are available at www.PluggedTheBook.com.

Golf: Golf is unlike other sports. There's no clock running down, no referee watching you play, or coach at the end of the bench. Your competitors aren't tackling you or applying a zone defense or trying to pick you off of first. In golf it's just you against the course. You also decide whether or not you're going to get to the course early to warm up. It's up to you to choose to practice or take lessons. It is the ultimate sport for taking personal responsibility for the outcome.

You are also responsible for how you treat others around you on the course. For example, if you're a foursome on a par three and a fast twosome is behind you, you should wave them on and let them play through. You're also responsible for raking the sand after you walk in it and repairing your ball marks on the green. Oh, yeah, and counting your strokes. *All of them*. Which includes every swing-and-a-miss.

The old adage is true: if you want to learn what someone is really like, play a round of golf with them. It's because the game is so challenging and there are so many ways to veer off the right path. At the end of the day, no golfer will think less of you if you shoot one hundred and two...but they will think less of you if you shoot one hundred and ten and say you broke a hundred.

Life: In the end, we are all judged by our character and the things we do. How we treat others. How hard we try. How much we drive our roommate's convertible when he's gone for the weekend and told us to not even back it out of the driveway.

Actions really do speak louder than words, and the only person who owns your actions is *you.* Ultimately, only you are responsible for who you are and what you do.

President Harry S. Truman knew he was responsible for the success of the nation and reminded himself with his famous "the buck stops here" sign on his desk. To succeed in whatever you do, you first have to come to the realization that it is up to you.

So grab the wheel and drive (unless it's your roommate's convertible), because in the end, where you end up on life's long and winding road is up to *you.*

# Post Game

Golf is an amazing game because you get to decide how you want to play it. Want more challenge? Tee off from the back tees. Not hitting your driver well? Pull out your three wood. Having problems pitching around the green with your sand wedge? Switch to a bump-and-run with your seven iron.

Business is much the same. There isn't only one way to sell, manage, or lead. T. Boone Pickens, Bill Gates, and Warren Buffett each have used a very different approach to achieve outstanding results.

The key to success is the ability to know where you want to go and have a way to get there. Shooting for PAR is a simple, proven methodology to help you do just that.

Prioritize. Focus on what matters most.
Adapt. See change as an opportunity.
Be Responsible. Take ownership of the outcome.

Make this PAR mindset an integral part of everything you do and you'll dramatically increase the likelihood you'll dig out of a tough situation, get the important things done, and ultimately succeed.

 **Discussion Points**

- Where are you or your company plugged? What are the indicators that show when someone or their company is stuck in the old ways of doing things?

- Overall, how did Chet handle the crisis with Trident? What would you have done differently?

- What could the AlphaMax team have done to avoid the competitive situation they found themselves in? How are you looking at your clients and competitive risks?

- What excuses did the AlphaMax team make? Were they valid? What excuses does your team make when things go awry?

- Chet's defining moment was turning in the putter during the tournament. What would you have done?

- What does the phrase "go back to the fundamentals" mean within the story? Did Chet take that approach? What are the most important fundamentals in your work that you need to prioritize?

- Reggie told Chet that "winners find a way to win." What might he mean by that statement?

What do you need to do differently in order to win?

- Chet started putting better when he began visualizing his putts going in. How can you apply this same concept to success in business and in your personal life? What does success look like? What behaviors and activities will get you there?

- What are the positives and negatives around Chet's purchase of an expensive putter?

- How important is it to get close and stay close to your customers? Was AlphaMax doing everything possible with their most important customer? What are you doing to keep your customers fully engaged with you?

- What was Chet's attitude and demeanor during the crisis conversations at AlphaMax, and how much of a factor was that attitude on the eventual outcome?

- Chet spoke to Trident about the gap between promises and execution. Did his comments ring true? Is your company trusted by your customers, suppliers, and employees to do the right thing? Are you? How do you know?

- Do you think Trident will stay with AlphaMax? Why or why not?

- Do you think Chet and Reggie won the tournament? Why or why not?

- Do you think Walt, AlphaMax's president, will be upset with Chet for committing to pay fifty-thousand dollars for Trident's software project? Did Chet overstep his bounds?

- What changes did Chet make on the golf course, and how much did they contribute to his improvement?

- Chet rallied his troops around a single objective: the need to hold on to their biggest customer. How might this situation have turned out had he not built customer-obsession among his entire company? Do you involve your entire team on key initiatives or just send an email stating your decision?

- If you could change three things that would immediately benefit your company, what would they be? What's stopping you from doing them tomorrow?

- Did Chet hold himself accountable for improving his golf game and keeping the Trident account? How do you hold yourself personally accountable for results?

- Chet used the PAR concepts during a crisis situation. What are the differences in prioritizing, adapting, and taking responsibility when times are relatively calm?

Additional discussion points specifically around PAR—Prioritize, Adapt, and Be Responsible—are available in the online "Are You a PAR Player?" assessment at www.PluggedTheBook.com.

Acknowledgments

Much like success in business, writing this book turned out to be a team sport. And we have an all-star cast to thank. The inspiration for the book came, a number of years ago, from a high school sophomore. Having finished his round in an important school golf tournament, the young man checked in at the scorer's table. There he discovered that his playing opponent had incorrectly listed his nine-hole shot total as a thirty-seven. (In high school you keep score for the person you are playing with.) By this time, his opponent had left the course and was on the bus heading home, so no one would have known that the score was wrong. "We need to change that because I actually shot a thirty-nine," he told the scorer. Changing the score meant his team didn't win that leg of a four-game match. That young man is our son, Andy Barr, and we've never been more proud of him. He also helped us with this book.

There are many other friends and associates who helped us with their time, feedback, and encouragement: Eleanor Barr, Rod Barr, Roderick W. Barr, Jodi Billerman, Ken Campbell, Ron Campbell, Willie Carden, Peter Davies, Steve Dilbone, Jim Dugan, Katie Durstock, Larry Drehs, P.B. Dye, John Eckberg, Scott Farmer, Crystal Faulkner, Paul Flory, Bill Goetz, Marshall Goldsmith, Holly Green, Scott Gregory, Andy Hawking, Jack Heffron, Irmgard Hehmann, Dr. Paul Hersey, Paul Higham, Jim Hrusovsky, Phil Huff, Richard Hunt, George Joseph, Ginger Kent, Steve Kent, Chip Klosterman, Glenna Kraus, Don Lane, Eddie Lehner, Jeremy Lott, Marty Lott, Sarah McArthur, John Mariotti, Heide Moser, Steve Olberding, Jim Pancero, Pierre Paroz, Brian Plummer, Dave Pollak, Todd Price, Mark Rentschler, Debra Riley, Jack Roehr, Sean Shafer, Rich Shurmer, Carol Shea, Tom Starr, Louie Strike, and Jim Wycoff.

Plugged-In

Free Online Tools

Visit www.PluggedTheBook.com to discover more ways to incorporate the ideas from *Plugged* into your business. Free downloads include the *Plugged* Scorecard (your guide to strategic thinking, including planning and implementation) and the Are You a PAR Player? Assessment (a measurement of your company and your team's strengths and weaknesses), plus much more.

Barr Corporate Success

Visit www.BarrCorporateSuccess.com to learn more about how co-author Krissi Barr's consulting firm can help your company dig out and get the right things done. Her proven services include strategic planning and implementation, assessments, coaching, and training.

Keynote Speech

Supercharge your next meeting with a keynote speech by Krissi Barr. Dynamic, energetic, and powerful, she will not only entertain but will deliver memorable takeaway value for all in attendance. Email her at Krissi@ BarrCorporateSuccess.com for more information.

Bulk Book Sales

Plug in your entire team! Quantity sales of *Plugged* are available at discounts to companies, associations, and other organizations. Books are also available with your personalized message on the cover. For more information, please contact Richard@ClerisyPress.com.

Plugged *Training*

Learn to apply the three specific tools for digging out and getting the right things done in your organization. Krissi Barr's training programs are geared to produce results for your business, your team, and your customers. You'll receive an assessment of where your organization needs to build, gain a deep understanding of how to apply the three tools in your organization, and work through actual situations that you'll bring to the class. You'll also walk away with new ways to achieve success, definitive action plans to start implementing the next day, and an ongoing process to ensure follow-through. Email Krissi@ BarrCorporateSuccess.com for more information.

Krissi and Dan Barr are dynamic business leaders who have been married for more than twenty-five years. Both are graduates of Miami University, where Krissi also earned her MBA.

Krissi is president and founder of Barr Corporate Success, a business consulting firm. Specializing in strategies to maximize profitability, her interdisciplinary approach to business draws from her extensive background. Her industry experience includes banking, telecom, international business, and manufacturing.

Dan is a senior executive at Cintas, a $3.9 billion business services company. He started his career with a family business and later spent eight years as an entrepreneur, cofounding an entertainment software company.

Both are avid golfers.